American Rally Action

Ronnie Arnold

SPEED-PICS Publishing

ISBN 10: 0-9778320-0-7
ISBN 13: 978-0-9778320-0-2
Library of Congress Control Number: 2006902504

Printed in China

Book design and production: Tabby House
Cover design: Juanita Dix
Cover background photos: Jupiter Images

SPEED-PICS Publishing
6101 Long Prairie Road, #744-110
Flower Mound, TX 75028
www.speed-pics.com

Contents

Appendices

Foreword by Wilson von Kessler

The opportunity to author a foreword to *American Rally Action*, is indeed an honor. When asked, the question arose as to what needed to be addressed, and there is much to address.

In late 2003, NASA Rally Sport was formed, with a vision of forward-looking, professional and safe events that were not the status quo at the time. After a successful 2004 developing regional events and series, the decision was reached to move forward with a national level series, the United States Rally Championship. This was not without trepidation, as NASA Rally Sport's focus has been from the start taking care of the clubman rallier, who forms the backbone of every single rally event that takes place in the United States.

In 2005, with the aid of our partners at the United States Auto Club, international stage rally in the United States came home to the club that sanctioned arguably the first modern-era stage event, the 1959 USAC American International Rally, which in turn was modeled on the events taking place in Europe at the time, including the famed Rallye de Monte Carlo. Nick Craw at ACCUS, FIA, and Rollie Helmling at USAC conferred the sporting authority of FIA rally in the United States to the championship, and we haven't looked back.

The decision was made to start slowly with events that were truly worthy of international stature. Cherokee Trails, New York, Rim of the World and the Ramada Express were the logical events to begin with, as all of them had significant and legitimate rally pedigree.

Moving from "outlaw" roots to presenting the official FIA sanctioned series in the United States is two years has been quite heady. 2006 promises even more. The championship has been expanded to eight events, with the addition of Prescott, Olympus, Rally Tennessee and an additional New York round. This includes two full tarmac rounds, a first in the United States for any national or international level series.

Obviously, this growth could not be achieved without the involvement of a number of individuals who should be recognized: First of all Ray and Donna Hocker, Roger and Lynette Allison, John Shirley and Kendall Russell who had the vision to form NASA Rally Sport; additionally, the organizers who have had the vision to join our effort, including Ivan and Olga Orisek, Michael Taylor, and Steve McQuaid; and most importantly, and coming full circle, our competitors and volunteers, who form the basis of the sport, and guarantee its continuing viability. There are many other valuable and import contributors to our success that in the interest of brevity have been left out, and I apologize in advance for these omissions.

At the risk of showing an East Coast bias, a special thanks needs to be given to the Irish ex-pat rally community, as their participation and support has led to excellent depth and competition at our events. Tom Lawless and Jason Gillespie, the 2005 USRC champions, are just but one of many fine teams who have graced our rallies with both their competitive spirit and their camaraderie.

Lastly, Ronnie Arnold needs to be thanked for the time and effort that he has expended in the compilation *American Rally Action*, hopefully the first of many.

WILSON VON KESSLER
U.S. RALLY CHAMPIONSHIP

Introduction

I was introduced to rallying before I was old enough to hold my driver's license when my brother-in-law persuaded me, with some friends, to help him marshal the Circuit of Ireland International Rally. We spent five days following the competitors around Ireland and I became hooked on the spectacle, the action and the car fumes.

Most rallies are held in out-of-the-way locations—forests, deserts and mountain tops are common. The drivers hurl their cars along narrow twisty roads as fast as they dare. They race against the clock not against each other. While the competitors go through, the roads—called stages—are closed to all other traffic and pedestrians. The stages are connected by "transit" roads—which are regular roads still open to the public, on which the drivers drive within the speed limits and obey all regulations.

It is partially that lack of side-by-side racing that allows the competitors to be traditionally more helpful to each other. It is common for teams to share parts and tools. And it is a requirement that a team must stop to give any other team in trouble assistance.

The only people crazier than the drivers are the co-drivers, who sit strapped into the passenger seat, trusting the driver to get them to the end of the event safely. The job of the co-driver is to navigate the team between stages and to call out "pace notes" while on the stages.

Over time I would compete, organize and report on many rallies; but at some indefinable point I took the twelve-step program and changed focus to build a career, and a living, in technology.

Skip forward about thirty years and I found myself in the United States spending too many hours in two-story office blocks talking about computers and software. One day I had a watercooler conversation with a friend about motor sport. He made a passing comment about those crazy people who take their cars out into the forests to race.

My heart skipped a beat. Did he mean "rallying"? Was there some chance that, in the land of NASCAR, there was also room for rallying? I went on the Internet and checked it out. A few months later I found myself standing in a forest, in the snow, watching rally cars again. My addiction had reasserted itself.

It was the 2004 season and I quickly learned that the sport in the United States had been going through a bruising time. The works teams had withdrawn and by the end of that year the sanctioning body, the SCCA, would also withdraw from the sport. The situation was bleak. And yet out of this, the sport would fight back arguably fitter than ever because from the one SCCA championship would be spawned two championships: the Rally America Championship and the United States Rally Championship. Both series are run by people who are dedicated to bringing new ideas and new enthusiasm to the sport in the United States.

The 2005 season would be the first season of this new structure. For the organizers there would be many challenges. For the competitors, there would be the opportunity to race on some of the best forest roads in the world. For the spectators, there would be the opportunity to watch in fascination as great competition unfolded in front of them.

The Rally America Championship included eight events. Starting in a subzero Michigan January with Sno*Drift and including visits to all parts of the country from Oregon to Maine, the story of the series would be the hard-fought duel between Canadian hero Pat Richard, co-driven by his sister Nathalie, and Swedish ex-world champion Stig Blomqvist with his co-driver Ana Goni. As the series progressed the lead for the championship would switch backwards and forwards until the final event on the edge of Lake Superior—just a few hundred miles from where it started ten months previously.

The U.S. Rally Championship would consist of four events. Two in California and two on the East Coast (New York and Tennessee). The headlines would be all about Tom Lawless and his co-driver Jason Gillespie dominating the series—winning all the events they entered. But the headlines would not give the full story as their victories were never assured and were determinedly fought by Seamus Burke, Peter Workum and Matthew Iorio.

In producing this book, my goal has been to make a record of the competition for the 2005 rally season in the United States. That meant covering all the events within the Rally America and U.S. Rally Championships. Due to space considerations, I had to decide to exclude some excellent regional events, such as the 100 Acre Wood, and regional championships, such as the East Coast Rally Championship. Maybe next time!

In 2005, the World Rally Championship visited León in México for the second time. Given my definition of the events to be included in this book, above, the WRC should not be here. But I will defend my decision to include it because, in my opinion, its color, action and proximity make it a "must-see" event for any American rally enthusiast.

This is the story of the drivers and co-drivers who competed for American rally championships told mainly in photographs.

I hope you enjoy it.

Acknowledgments

When I decided to produce this book I did not realize how big a challenge I was undertaking. Collecting and collating the data, reports and images has been a much greater task than I had ever expected.

I have made every effort to ensure accuracy throughout the book but, being human, I am sure that errors have crept in. All errors are mine and mine alone.

Throughout the season I took in the region of 20,000 photographs. The volume of images—and the desire for quality—has made it a challenge to get to a shortlist for the book. I have tried to spread the halo as wide as possible but inevitably there are many skilled teams whose spectacular exploits I have been unable to include. I will try to do better next time.

My thanks to all the great enthusiasts who work with the individual events, Rally America, the U.S. Rally Association and the World Rally Championship. Throughout the season they have all been generous in helping me when I visit events and, during the production of this book, they have handled my frequent strange requests with patience and enthusiasm. I thank them for their permission to reproduce their logos and the event and championship results. Their copyright is hereby recognized.

Also, my thanks to the competitors who, throughout the season, put up with having me stick my camera lens through their car window; or find me standing on the outside of a blind corner, or just over the crest on a flat-out jump. It is always my goal to record the action without affecting it.

I also want to thank the photographers who contributed additional material to this book: Lorne Trezise and Matthew Simmons.

The book could never have been produced without the experienced assistance of Jim and Linda Salisbury of Tabby House. Their experience of the process of getting from a blank page to a bound document was invaluable.

Otis Dimiters / Peter Monin dig into the snow.

SNO*DRIFT RALLY
Atlanta, Michigan
January 28–29, 2005

Ken Block / Christian Edstrom pass the spectator area on stage 13.

Sno*Drift was the first round of the 2005 rally season. Last year's SCCA champions, Pat Richard and Nathalie Richard were favorites to repeat Pat's Sno*Drift win from last year. The main competition was expected to be from Seamus Burke with co-driver Jason Gillespie.

In some ways the conditions were good—no snow had been forecast and the temperatures during the day were not much below freezing. But the corollary was that there was little snow on the roads, so the cars had to get their traction from the underlying ice. As most stages were used more than once, the ice would become polished and treacherous.

The event started on Friday afternoon with four stages in a loop to the east of Lewiston, bringing the competitors back to Lewiston for the service and preparation for the three night stages that would conclude day one of the event.

The first stage was a short, mainly downhill stage. It would be a good test of tire grip. Richard took the fastest time—covering the two miles in exactly two minutes. Five seconds behind him were Jonathan

Chris Whiteman / Mike Rossey . . .

Bottoms / Carolyn Bosley (Subaru); followed closely by Mark Utecht / Rob Bohn (Subaru).

Despite its length, King Scenic managed to catch Daniel Adamson / Jason Takkunen in their Saturn when they left the road, losing twelve minutes, near the finish.

The second stage, East Fish Lake—the most southerly of the event—comprised several roads sweeping west to east making a total length of ten miles. Richard was able to extend his lead over Burke by two seconds. He was enjoying the battle and described it as a "good close tussle."

This time it was the turn of Larry Parker / Ray Summers to meet the snowbanks in their Eagle Talon. They lost thirty minutes but were able to continue.

Stage 3 (The Ranch) is a mixture of public and private roads. It is a tight, technical and, in places, rough stage. Yet, despite its short distance, many of the competitors were overshooting corners and some even got lost when the banners marking the roads were taken down by earlier competitor's mistakes.

William Bacon / Peter Watt (Subaru) lost thirty minutes and Otis Dimiters / Peter Monin (Subaru) lost twenty minutes.

Once again Richard took top honors, but this time there was a clear demonstration of his potential domination of the event as he cleared the stage forty-three seconds ahead of rival Burke.

Stage 4, a fast run along the side of Avery Lake—took the competitors back to service. Richard stretched his lead over Burke by a further two seconds.

*Pat Richard / Nathalie Richard drive
into the night on day one.*

. . . make full use of the snowbanks.

After Service, Richard continued to build his lead on stage 5 but, as night closed in and temperatures plunged, Burke started to fight back—taking fastest times on six and seven.

As the crews headed back to their hotels, Richard held a lead of thirty-three seconds over Burke. A full two minutes behind Burke, were Matthew Iorio / Ole Holter (Subaru) who were in their own private battle for third place with Chris Gilligan / Joe Petersen (Mitsubishi)—just sixteen seconds separating the two teams.

Ten stages were scheduled for the second day. The first, stage 8, was the narrow and twisty Hardwood stage just south of Atlanta.

The longest stage of the event—at twenty-five miles—was stage 9. It was an amalgam of the roads that would form stages 11 and 12 later in the day. But this time the stage was continuous—making it a test of concentration for the competitors.

Burke was determined to continue his speed from last night but as he approached the end of the stage—a 600-yard straight into a fast right—he lost control of

his Mitsubishi, hitting a tree on the right-hand side then swinging round to block the road. Both Burke and co-driver Gillespie were fine, but the stage had to be cancelled due to the time it took to clear the blockage.

Burke's demise left Richard with a clear lead over newly promoted Iorio in second

Matt Bushore / Andy Bushore have to dig themselves out of the snowbank.

*Doug Shepherd and
Rob Bohn check
stage times at service.*

place and Gilligan in third. With almost four minutes in hand, the task became one of keeping between the snow banks while maintaining his position.

After a service halt the teams tackled stage 10: a group of fast hilly roads south of town. Richard took fastest time with Bacon second, fourteen seconds back.

Stages 11 and 12 were a repeat of 9. This time there were no problems and the times were good. Richard winning stage 11 from Bacon and stage 12 from Henry Krolikowski / Cindy Krolikowski (Subaru).

Thirteen was a short stage close to town and won again by Richard, who consolidated his dominance by taking the next four stages. Behind him Bacon was leading the pack although, due to his thirty-minute error on stage 3, he was out of contention for the event. Dimiters was in the same situation posting fast times on all the remaining stages, but it was Iorio whose steady progress throughout the event gave him second place.

Class wins went to Tanner Foust / Scott Crouch (PGT), Doug Shepherd / Bob Martin (Group 5), Don Jankowski and Ken Nowak (Production) and Matt Johnston / Alex Kihurani (Group 2).

The overall result was an easy win for Pat Richard and his co-driver sister, Nathalie. They also took the Group N win. Second place, and Open Class, went to Matthew Iorio / Ole Holter—Iorio's best national result to date.

Chris Whiteman / Mike Rossey.

Event chairman Don Rathgeber holds the control board hit by Seamus Burke on Stage 9

Jonathan Bottoms / Carolyn Bosley on Stage 2.

The event mascot gives a hand.

Pat Richard at service.

High-minded spectators.

John Cirisan / Josh Hamacher would retire after Stage 9.

William Bacon / Peter Watt work for the camera.

Sno*Drift Rally Schedule

Stage #	First Car	Stage Name
Friday, January 28		
	15:01	Rally Start
1	15:14	King Scenic
2	15:42	East Fish Lake
3	16:15	The Ranch 1
4	17:03	Avery Lake
	Service	
5	19:03	The Ranch 2
6	19:37	Greasy Creek
7	20:18	Shoreline
Saturday, January 29		
8	9:15	Hardwood Hard
9	9:50	That Old Black River
10	12:21	The Hunters
11	12:55	Old State
12	13:08	Black River
13	13:59	Hungry Five 1
	Service	
14	16:27	Hardwood Easy
15	17:06	McCormick Lake
16	17:46	Hungry Five 2
17	18:26	Thunder River
	19:04	Rally Finish

Above: Seamus Burke / Jason Gillespie hold a strong second place until their spectacular off on stage 9.

Below: Tanner Foust / Scott Crouch at the spectator area.

Sno*Drift Rally Results

O'all	Class	Class	Car #	Driver / Co-Driver	Car	SS-1	SS-2	SS-3	SS-4	SS-5	SS-6	SS-7	SS-8	SS-9	SS-10	SS-11	SS-12	SS-13	SS-14	SS-15	SS-16	SS-17	Road Penalties	Total
1	1	GN	1	Patrick Richard / Nathalie Richard	2002 Subaru WRX Sti	02:00.0	09:53.7	10:20.9	05:36.1	10:56.2	10:47.1	05:35.7	04:41.0	0	08:10.6	07:47.4	15:36.7	03:31.6	04:52.6	08:15.7	03:37.9	06:01.6		1:57:44.8
2	1	O	99	Matthew Iorio / Ole Holter	2001 Subaru Impreza	02:10.6	10:21.7	11:19.6	05:57.9	11:40.9	10:55.2	05:51.0	05:05.6	0	08:32.7	08:18.1	16:43.0	03:54.3	05:07.6	08:43.5	04:02.1	06:11.8		2:04:55.6
3	2	O	27	Chris Gilligan / Joe Petersen	1997 Mitsubishi EVO IV	02:14.3	10:19.0	11:17.2	05:50.0	11:50.6	10:59.7	06:02.2	05:41.3	0	08:38.8	08:22.5	16:31.4	03:50.1	05:07.6	08:36.9	03:58.9	06:12.4		2:05:32.9
4	2	GN	91	Jonathan Bottoms / Carolyn Bosley	2002 Subaru WRX	02:05.4	10:19.6	11:08.5	05:50.1	11:54.9	11:08.2	06:25.0	05:00.3	0	08:41.7	08:15.8	17:15.4	03:59.1	05:11.9	08:40.0	03:52.6	06:12.7		2:06:01.2
5	3	GN	44	Henry Krolikowski / Cindy Krolikowski	2000 Subaru WRX STi	02:09.1	10:40.7	11:33.2	06:07.5	12:06.6	11:26.5	06:05.2	05:08.6	0	09:15.2	08:43.8	15:55.2	04:02.3	05:18.1	08:59.2	04:17.4	06:40.7		2:08:29.3
6	4	GN	83	Mark Utecht / Rob Bohn	2002 Subaru WRX	02:05.7	10:18.2	11:08.5	05:38.7	17:15.9	11:11.1	05:51.2	04:57.3	0	08:29.5	08:33.4	16:27.3	03:49.1	05:02.2	08:34.2	03:49.0	06:05.3		2:09:19.6
7	5	GN	43	Ken Block / Christian Edstrom	2004 Subaru WRX STi	02:20.1	11:58.1	12:31.4	06:12.1	12:17.4	11:26.7	06:17.3	05:17.6	0	08:50.9	08:17.4	16:32.0	03:52.6	05:09.1	08:41.6	04:00.2	06:23.2		2:10:07.7
8	1	PGT	429	Tanner Foust / Scott Crouch	2002 Subaru WRX	02:09.4	10:50.4	11:21.7	05:57.7	12:45.8	11:30.0	06:13.6	05:06.4	0	09:03.6	08:26.8	17:35.3	04:03.5	05:16.4	08:56.6	04:09.3	07:06.5		2:10:33.0
9	1	G5	52	Doug Shepherd / Bob Martin	2005 Dodge SRT4	02:20.5	11:01.9	11:41.5	06:10.2	12:24.7	11:46.7	06:13.0	05:07.5	0	09:03.7	08:46.4	17:31.0	03:59.4	05:18.5	08:52.8	04:08.3	06:34.8		2:11:00.9
10	3	O	508	Tom Ottey / Pam McGarvey	1989 Mazda 323 GTX	02:12.5	11:20.0	11:57.9	05:55.5	12:05.4	11:24.0	06:12.3	05:12.6	0	08:40.2	09:04.5	18:19.0	04:05.3	05:21.5	08:48.9	04:00.8	06:27.7		2:11:08.1
11	2	G5	143	Chris Whiteman / Mike Rossey	2004 Dodge SRT4	02:22.4	11:44.7	12:53.3	06:29.8	12:42.2	12:42.5	06:36.3	05:25.2	0	09:30.9	09:11.9	18:21.7	04:20.5	05:52.3	09:49.6	04:26.2	07:08.7		2:19:37.2
12	2	PGT	153	Eric Langbein / Jeremy Wimpey	1988 Toyota All-Trac	02:19.1	11:21.0	12:16.8	06:05.6	12:11.6	11:02.8	05:58.5	13:40.0	0	09:07.2	08:55.2	16:13.4	04:04.1	05:26.8	08:53.3	04:13.3	06:24.6	02:48.0	2:21:02.3
13	3	G5	42	Eric Burmeister / Dave Shindle	2003 Mazda Protege	02:23.3	11:45.9	12:21.2	06:33.1	12:33.4	12:08.2	06:33.5	05:37.1	0	09:38.7	09:13.7	18:42.9	04:14.8	05:48.0	09:44.4	04:28.3	06:49.7	04:30.0	2:23:06.2
14	4	O	558	Jim Cox / Mark Larson	2004 Chevrolet S10	02:50.2	13:14.7	13:30.2	06:48.2	13:43.8	13:43.1	07:13.9	05:40.6	0	10:30.7	09:58.9	19:53.9	04:37.6	06:17.5	10:32.5	04:57.0	07:47.1	01:00.0	2:32:19.9
15	1	P	53	Don Jankowski / Ken Nowak	2001 Dodge Neon ACR	02:30.5	12:10.6	17:02.2	06:37.2	13:05.7	15:30.6	06:54.7	05:52.6	0	10:04.9	09:35.0	20:07.5	04:44.0	06:12.7	10:05.3	04:38.2	07:20.0		2:32:31.7
16	4	G5	60	Bruce Davis / Jimmy Brandt	2000 Dodge Neon	02:46.2	13:01.9	14:00.3	07:11.9	13:48.9	13:48.0	07:11.4	06:04.9	0	10:58.6	10:40.8	21:28.5	04:43.5	06:34.3	11:00.2	05:06.0	08:00.2		2:36:25.6
17	6	GN	947	William Bacon / Peter Watt	2004 Subaru STi	02:15.3	10:34.6	43:59.4	06:21.6	12:34.6	11:35.6	06:11.6	04:50.0	0	08:24.9	07:50.5	16:20.3	03:42.4	05:01.3	08:26.3	03:49.3	06:02.5		2:38:00.2
18	7	GN	774	Otis Dimiters / Peter Monin	2002 Subaru WRX STi	02:06.4	10:59.0	33:19.6	06:01.8	11:40.3	11:05.0	12:36.2	04:51.9	0	08:31.3	08:24.8	16:20.2	04:41.8	05:04.2	08:38.1	03:55.3	06:09.3	04:30.0	2:38:55.2
19	3	PGT	82	Joan Hoskinson / Jeff Secor	2000 Subaru Impreza RS	03:00.3	13:47.1	16:37.7	07:49.9	15:19.6	14:01.4	07:22.3	05:57.4	0	11:16.0	10:26.2	20:59.5	04:57.8	06:40.3	11:32.7	05:20.4	07:55.9		2:43:04.5
20	2	P	543	Mike Merbach / Jeff Feldt	1990 Volkswagon Jetta	02:37.5	13:17.9	14:33.3	07:14.4	21:08.8	18:52.3	06:29.6	06:30.9	0	11:44.0	10:12.0	20:28.0	04:53.4	06:36.1	11:03.4	05:03.4	07:47.5		2:48:31.5
21	1	G2	587	Matt Johnston / Alex Kihurani	1992 honda Civic	02:45.6	14:21.4	15:23.5	07:48.2	15:02.5	16:51.4	07:53.2	07:02.3	0	12:00.6	11:33.7	22:35.6	05:08.9	07:30.4	12:02.5	05:30.6	08:42.8		2:52:13.2
		O	25	Seamus Burke / Jason Gillespie	2003 Mitsubishi Evo VIII	02:09.2	09:55.6	11:03.1	05:38.3	11:17.9	10:09.8	05:29.6												DNF
		O	78	Mark Podoluch / Kazimierz Pudelek	1993 Subaru Impreza	02:22.3	12:42.4	13:27.8	06:45.0	13:24.2														DNF
		PGT	93	Bob Olson / Conrad Ketelsen	1999 Subaru RS 2.5																			DNF
		PGT	59	Patrick Moro / Ryan Johnson	2002 Subaru WRX																			DNF

Pat Richard / Nathalie Richard on their way to their first win of the season.

Marcus Grönholm / Timo Rautiainen (Peugeot) place second in the event.

CORONA
RALLY MÉXICO

León, México
March 11–13, 2005

The World Rally Championship visited León for the third round of the 2005 series.

The only American entry came from Wyeth Gubelmann and Cynthia Krolikowski, but they had to withdraw because their car was not ready in time for the start.

As last year, the Corona Rally México was a great spectacle. Petter Solberg and Phil Mills in their Subaru took a popular win over the Peugeots of Marcus Grönholm / Timo Rautiainen and Markko Märtin / Michael Park. In fourth place were world champions, Sébastien Loeb / Daniel Elena in a Citroën.

Ricardo Trivino, in a Peugeot 206, was the highest placed local driver with co-driver Carlos del Barrio.

Erwin Richter / Rafael Tellaeche (Mitsubishi) take the jump.

Petter Solberg / Phil Mills (Subaru) are waved on by their supporters.

Jani Paasonen / Jani Vainikka
(Skoda) kick the dust.

Markko Märtin / Michael Park.

*Armin Schwarz / Klaus Wicha (Skoda)
have a hard landing at the jump.*

*Chris Atkinson / Glenn MacNeall
(Subaru) on an early stage are fully
committed but have to retire later.*

World champions Sebastien Loeb / Daniel Elena through the water.

Guy Wilks / Phil Pugh from the U.K. won Class 6.

Rally fans enjoy the competition.

Armin Schwarz / Klaus Wicha round a turn.

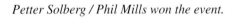

Petter Solberg / Phil Mills won the event.

*François Duval / Stéphanie Prevot would
retire in their Citroen.*

*Javier Ortuno / Juan Paulo López
(Peugeot 206) take the water.*

*Photographers capture Per-Gunnar
Andersson / Jonas Andersson
(Suzuki Ignis) flying high.*

Above left: Toni Gardemeister / Jakke Honkanen in the lead Ford Focus.

Above: Sébastien Loeb / Daniel Elena (Citroen) climb to a fourth overall.

Left: Harri Rovanperä / Risto Pietilainen (Mitsubishi) on their way to fifth overall.

Corona Rally México Schedule

Stage #	First Car	Stage Name	Kms
Friday, March 11			
	8:30	Rally Start	
1	9:07	Ibarilla - El Zauco 1	22.56
2	10:25	Ortega - La Esperanza 1	29.06
3	11:16	Santana - Cubilete 1	21.80
	13:01	Service	
4	14:08	Ibarilla - El Zauco 2	22.56
5	15:26	Ortega - La Esperanza 2	29.06
6	16:17	Santana - Cubilete 2	21.80
	17:37	Park Fermé	
Saturday, March 12			
	8:30	Day Start	
7	9:43	El Zauco - Mesa 1	25.45
8	11:06	Duarte - Otates 1	24.23
9	11:57	Derramadero - Chichimequillas 1	23.56
	13:37	Service	
10	15:10	El Zauco - Mesa 2	25.45
11	16:33	Duarte - Otates 2	24.23
12	17:24	Derramadero - Chichimequillas 2	23.56
	18:39	Park Fermé	
Sunday, March 13			
	8:30	Day Start	
13	9:17	Comanjilla - Chichimequillas	18.26
14	10:25	Alfaro - El Establo	44.39
	12:10	Rally Finish	

Marcus Grönholm / Timo Rautiainen (Peugeot) climb through the mountains.

Corona Rally México Results

POSITION	Group	Class	Car #	Driver		Co-Driver		Car	Total
1	A	8	5	Petter Solberg	N	Phil Mills	GB	Subaru Impreza WRC	3:41:06.2
2	A	8	7	Marcus Grönholm	Fin	Timo Rautiainen	Fin	Peugeot 307 WRC	3:41:40.7
3	A	8	8	Markko Märtin	EE	Michael Park	GB	Peugeot 307 WRC	3:42:44.5
4	A	8	1	Sébastien Loeb	F	Daniel Elena	MC	Citroën Xsara WRC	3:44:37.3
5	A	8	9	Harri Rovanperä	Fin	Risto Pietilainen	Fin	Mitsubishi Lancer WRC	3:43:44.3
6	A	8	3	Toni Gardemeister	Fin	Jakke Honkanen	Fin	Ford Focus RS WRC	3:45:11.8
7	A	8	15	Anthony Warmbold	D	Michael Orr	GB	Ford Focus RS WRC	3:47:07.2
8	A	8	10	Gilles Panizzi	F	Hervé Panizzi	F	Mitsubishi Lancer WRC	3:46:47.9
9	A	8	11	Armin Schwarz	D	Klaus Wicha	D	Skoda Fabia WRC	3:49:11.5
10	A	8	17	Xavier Pons	E	Oriol Julia	E	Peugeot 206 WRC	3:59:55.2
11	A	6	32	Guy Wilks	GB	Phil Pugh	GB	Suzuki Ignis	4:00:30.1
12	A	8	18	Ricardo Trivino	Mex	Carlos del Barrio	E	Peugeot 206 WRC	4:04:05.7
13	A	8	12	Jani Paasonen	Fin	Jani Vainikka	Fin	Skoda Fabia WRC	4:10:11.0
14	A	6	31	Per-Gunnar Andersson	S	Jonas Andersson	S	Suzuki Ignis	4:12:04.4
15	N	4	62	Michael Kahlfuss	D	Ronald Bauer	D	Mitsubishi Lancer Evo	4:26:26.9
16	N	4	61	Erwin Richter	Mex	Rafael Tellaeche	Mex	Mitsubishi Lancer Evo	4:28:50.9
17	A	6	39	Luca Cecchetini	I	Massimo Daddoveri	I	Renault Clio	4:30:12.1
18	N	4	64	Carlos Tejada	Mex	Hugo Ruiz	Mex	Mitsubishi Lancer Evo	4:39:19.8
19	A	6	42	Pavel Valousek	CZ	Pierangelo Scalvini	I	Suzuki Ignis	4:39:22.1
20	A	6	67	Omar Barquet	Mex	Raul Villareal	Mex	Peugeot 206 XS	5:11:39.6
21	A	6	72	Adrián Díaz Caneja	Mex	Fernando Name	Mex	Peugeot 206 XS	5:12:40.6
22	A	6	75	Juan Guichard	Mex	Daniel Alcalá	Mex	Peugeot 206 XS	5:15:29.6
23	A	6	81	Javier Ortuno	Mex	Juan Paulo López	Mex	Peugeot 206 XS	5:22:19.5
24	A	6	79	Armando Rodríguez	Mex	Fabian Islas	Mex	Peugeot 206 XS	5:26:14.4
25	A	6	76	Joan Casas	Mex	Luis Arciga	Mex	Peugeot 206 XS	5:29:57.8
26	A	6	77	Rogelio Martínez	Mex	Eduardo Naranjo	Mex	Peugeot 206 XS	5:30:30.5
27	A	6	80	Roberto Gnecchi	Mex	Delia López	Mex	Peugeot 206 XS	5:35:55.6
28	A	6	73	Oscar Uribe	Mex	Diego Rivas	Mex	Peugeot 206 XS	5:43:25.7

	Group	Class	Car #	Driver		Co-Driver		Car	Total
	A	8	2	François Duval	B	Stéphane Prevot	B	Citroën Xsara WRC	DNF
	A	8	4	Dani Sola	E	Xavier Amigo	E	Ford Focus RS WRC	DNF
	A	8	6	Chris Atkinson	Aus	Glenn MacNeall	Aus	Subaru Impreza WRC	DNF
	A	8	14	Roman Kresta	CZ	Jan Mozny	CZ	Ford Focus RS WRC	DNF
	A	8	16	Tobias Johansson	S	Old Floene	N	Subaru Impreza WRC	DNF
	A	6	40	Conrad Rautenbach	Zim	Carl Williamson	GB	Citroen Saxo	DNF
	N	4	63	Wyeth Gubelmann	USA	Cynthia Krolikowski	USA	Subaru Impreza WRX STI	DNF
	N	4	65	Antonio Alatorre	Mex	Braulio Contreras	Mex	Mitsubishi Lancer Evo	DNF
	A	6	66	Guerlain Chicherit	F	Matthieu Baumel	F	Fiat Punto	DNF
	A	6	68	Omar Chávez	Mex	Francisco Peniche	Mex	Peugeot 206 XS	DNF
	A	6	69	Mauricio Moreno	EC	Diego Fernández	EC	Peugeot 206 XS	DNF
	A	6	70	Sergio Ramirez	Mex	Eduardo López Negrete	Mex	Peugeot 206 XS	DNF
	A	6	71	Francisco Name	Mex	Horacio Chousal	Mex	Peugeot 206 XS	DNF
	A	6	74	Kurt Richter	Mex	Agustin Acevedo	Mex	Peugeot 206 XS	DNF
	A	6	78	Erik Karam	Mex	Ignacio Moreno	Mex	Peugeot 206 XS	DNF
	A	6	82	Andrés Giesmann	Mex	Carlos Mauer	Mex	Peugeot 206 XS	DNF

A Peugeot climbs the Guanajuato mountains.

Spectators watch Josh Chang / Alex Kihurani.

CHEROKEE TRAILS INTERNATIONAL RALLY

Chattanooga, Tennessee
March 18–19, 2005

The first round of the 2005 U.S. Rally Championship series was held in the scenic Cherokee National Forest outside Chattanooga, Tennessee.

The event would provide twelve stages with 110 miles of competition over two days.

As befits an event held the day after St. Patrick's day, there was a strong Irish entry including Tom Lawless / Jason Gillespie in a Mitsubishi and Seamus Burke / Eddie Fries in a Libra Racing Hyundai Tiburon. Other entries of interest included John Buffum—eleven times U.S. Rally Champion driving another Libra Racing Hyundai—with co-driver Mark Williams and Peter Workum / Chrissie Beavis in an Autosport Engineering Subaru.

The first day included four stages Parksville and Iron Ore were each run two times. Lawless took fastest time on stage 1 with Buffum

Tom Lawless / Jason Gillespie drive to a clear first place.

Bruce Davis / Jim Brandt in their Dodge Neon.

*Martin Donnelly / Charlie Bradley catch
Donald Kennedy / Keith Kennedy. The
Kennedys would go on to take eighth overall.*

*Patrick Lilly / Bernard Farrell
take fourth overall.*

Cherokee Trails International Rally Schedule

Stage #	First Car	Stage Name	Miles
Friday, March 18			
	16:00	Rally Start	
1	16:25	Parksville 1	9.00
2	16:52	Iron Ore 1	7.57
	17:19	Service	
3	18:14	Parksville 2	9.00
4	18:41	Iron Ore 2	7.57
Saturday, March 19			
5	8:14	Sina Branch 1	7.98
6	8:38	Blue Ridge 1	7.60
	9:43	Service	
7	11:11	Clear Creek 1	5.64
8	12:07	Indian Creek 1	17.57
	12:59	Service	
9	14:13	Sina Branch 2	7.98
10	14:37	Blue Ridge 2	7.60
	15:42	Service	
11	17:10	Clear Creek 2	5.64
12	18:06	Indian Creek 2	17.57
	19:13	Rally Finish	

Matt Iorio / Ole Holter take third overall.

Cherokee Trails Rally Results

O'all	Class	Class	Car #	Driver / Co-Driver	Car	SS-1	SS-2	SS-3	SS-4	SS-6	SS-7	SS-8	SS-9	SS-10	SS-11	SS-12	SS-13	SS-14	SS-15	SS-16	SS-17	SS-18	SS-19	Road Penalties	Total
1	1	GN	65	Stig Blomqvist / Ana Goni	Subaru STi WRX	01:32	02:16	01:35	02:09	05:27	13:39	08:25	09:02	07:29	13:42	08:27	09:09	06:07	11:20	11:16	10:16	11:15	10:59		2:24:05.3
2	2	GN	199	Travis Pastrana / Christian Edstrom	Subaru WRX STi	01:36	02:14	01:39	02:10	05:17	14:00	08:25	09:13	07:34	13:50	08:23	09:11	06:07	11:36	11:23	10:21	11:16	11:06		2:25:21.6
3	1	O	39	Carl Jardevall / Amity Trowbridge	Mitsubishi Evo	01:33	02:19	01:35	02:12	05:28	13:56	08:23	09:24	07:42	14:02	08:31	09:16	06:06	11:42	11:43	10:34	11:21	11:04		2:26:51.0
4	2	O	99	Matt Iorio / Ole Holter	Subaru Impreza	01:33	02:38	01:39	02:14	05:22	14:40	08:47	09:32	07:50	14:20	08:47	09:26	06:16	11:40	11:32	10:40	11:39	11:30		2:30:04.0
5	3	GN	103	Wyeth Gubelmann / Cindy Krolikowski	Subaru Impreza	01:34	02:23	01:36	02:17	05:19	14:15	08:57	09:50	07:49	14:17	08:51	09:39	06:19	12:19	11:58	10:45	11:49	11:42		2:31:39.3
6	4	GN	947	William Bacon / Peter Watt	Subaru Impreza	01:35	02:21	01:37	02:14	05:29	14:07	11:17	10:02	08:10	14:01	08:26	09:16	05:55	11:44	11:35	10:35	11:13	11:11	02:00.0	2:32:47.5
7	1	PGT	616	Norman LeBlanc / Keith Morison	Subaru Impreza WRX	01:38	02:22	01:44	02:16	05:40	14:38	08:51	09:51	08:47	14:46	08:54	09:38	06:19	12:01	11:44	11:06	11:48	11:35		2:33:39.6
8	5	GN	774	Otis Dimiters / Peter Monin	Subaru WRX STi	01:33	02:23	01:37	02:13	05:41	14:55	09:03	10:08	08:17	14:51	09:00	09:55	06:18	11:53	12:03	10:38	11:52	11:34		2:33:54.3
9	2	PGT	429	Tanner Foust / Scott Crouch	Subaru WRX	01:31	02:23	01:37	02:15	05:39	14:44	09:02	09:58	08:09	14:59	09:03	10:15	06:40	12:12	12:00	10:53	11:49	11:50		2:34:59.2
10	3	PGT	46	Matthew Johnson / Wendy Nakamoto	Subaru WRX	01:39	02:28	01:40	02:14	05:40	14:56	09:09	10:09	08:06	15:07	09:21	10:11	06:20	12:28	12:08	11:04	12:08	11:45	48	2:37:20.7
11	6	GN	676	Mark McElduff / Damien Irwin	Subaru WRX Sti	01:40	02:28	01:44	02:21	05:54	14:50	08:58	10:14	08:16	14:58	09:02	10:06	06:37	12:52	12:19	11:07	12:22	11:52		2:37:41.3
12	4	PGT	153	Eric Langbein / Jeremy Wimpey	Toyota Celica	01:37	02:47	01:42	02:29	05:57	15:28	09:14	10:49	08:20	15:22	09:14	10:06	06:45	12:37	13:00	11:20	12:05	11:48		2:40:41.6
13	3	O	288	Gary Cavett / John Dillon	Subaru Impreza	01:33	02:24	01:39	02:18	05:53	14:43	09:05	10:05	08:37	15:13	09:13	10:01	06:31	12:24	12:14	10:59	13:04	17:12		2:43:07.1
14	4	O	252	Bob Trinder / Adam Trinder	Subaru WRX	01:33	02:40	01:38	02:23	05:59	15:41	09:41	10:36	08:32	15:39	09:39	10:26	06:55	13:00	12:38	11:32	13:04	12:02		2:43:38.6
15	5	O	227	Derik Nelson / John Allen	Mitsubishi Evo 8	01:43	02:30	01:44	02:23	06:18	16:01	09:42	10:29	08:36	16:01	09:54	10:51	06:59	12:43	12:26	11:28	12:27	12:15		2:44:31.2
16	7	GN	43	Ken Block / Alex Gelsomino	Subaru WRX Sti	01:38	02:18	01:40	02:11	05:29	14:09	08:37	09:20	07:42	14:21	08:51	09:40	06:15	11:38	26:29	10:52	11:39	11:44	01:36.0	2:46:09.4
17	1	P	232	Mark Tabor / Kevin Poirier	Acura RSX Type S	01:46	02:38	01:50	02:32	06:15	16:28	10:07	11:12	09:24	16:51	10:38	11:39	07:17	13:47	13:28	12:22	13:04	12:45		2:54:04.6
18	6	O	558	Jim Cox / Tim Sardelich	Chevrolet S10	01:41	02:30	01:52	02:35	06:33	17:13	10:23	11:25	09:22	16:39	10:32	11:32	07:29	13:36	13:05	12:52	13:04	13:53		2:56:15.7
19	2	P	49	Sans Thompson / Craig Marr	Dodge Neon	01:44	02:40	01:47	02:48	06:42	17:10	10:26	11:59	09:41	17:19	10:15	11:52	07:39	14:43	13:47	12:42	13:04	13:41	12	3:00:09.0
20	7	O	14	Amy BeberVanzo / Claire Chizma	Mitsubishi Evo 8	01:52	02:50	01:59	02:41	06:35	17:08	10:38	12:12	09:42	17:42	11:03	12:08	07:52	13:47	13:41	12:35	13:04	13:29		3:00:58.2
21	3	P	231	April Smith / Jeff Zurschmeide	Geo Metro	02:11	03:18	02:14	03:01	07:23	20:29	11:43	13:12	11:26	21:22	12:30	13:51	09:41	16:33	15:31	13:19	13:04	14:44		3:25:32.2
		PGT	215	Jamie Thomas / Matt Gauger	Subaru WRX Wagon	01:40	02:27	01:45	02:21	05:45	15:10	09:02	10:02	08:15	15:06	09:09	10:02	06:34	12:30	11:53	10:57				DNF
		PGT	866	Timothy Penasack / Rob McLelland	Subaru WRX	01:40	02:38	01:44	02:28	06:23	15:58	09:28	10:41	08:46	15:51	09:34	10:39	07:43	13:06	56:09					DNF
		G2	292	Derek Bottles / Jason Grahn	VW Golf	01:43	02:31	01:46	02:29	06:02	15:27	09:12	10:16	08:31	15:26	09:26									DNF
		GN	1	Pat Richard / Nathalie Richard	Subaru WRX	01:54	02:19	01:39	02:14	05:29	13:50	08:19	08:59	07:17											DNF
		O	207	Dave Hintz / Rick Hintz	Subaru WRX	01:35	02:35	01:39	02:19	05:44	15:07	09:15	09:58	08:11											DNF
		GN	600	Fintan McCarthy / Matthews Collins	Subaru WRX STi	01:44	02:50	01:45	02:35	06:08	15:18	09:01	10:05	08:15											DNF
		G5	60	Bruce Davis / Jimmy Brandt	Dodge SRT4	01:37	02:34	01:41	02:25	06:24	16:31	10:14	11:26	08:59											DNF
		PGT	323	Stephan Verdier / Allan Walker	Subaru WRX	01:34	02:20	01:35	02:15	05:26	14:16	09:45													DNF
		O	30	George Plsek / Jeff Burmeister	Mitsubishi Evo	01:32	02:08	01:37	02:14	05:55	16:44														DNF

Eric Heitkamp / Andrew Jessup take the hairpin in an Acura RSX.

Pat Richard / Nathalie Richard on stage 8.

OREGON TRAIL RALLY

Hillsboro, Oregon

April 22–24, 2005

Ben Wellermeyer / Rob Wellermeyer in the dusk.

After the snows and ice of a Michigan January, the Rally America championship moved to the rains of an Oregon spring. The second round of the championship was headquartered in Hillsboro, just to the west of Portland.

This was the first event of the season that included an entry from David Sutton's UK-based team. Their Bodega Otazu sponsored Subaru WRX was being driven by 1984 World Champion, Stig Blomqvist and his co-driver Ana Goni. The big question in everyone's mind was how would the competition between Stig and Pat Richard resolve.

The Oregon Trail is unusual for the United States being a three-day event. The Friday included five spectator stages all within the Portland International Speedway on a clear and cool evening.

The first stage did not answer the question as Richard snapped a drive shaft on the start line and ended the stage in second last

Top: Matthew Johnson / Wendy Nakamoto turn onto the back straightaway of the Super Special.

place. Tanner Foust / Scott Crouch were fastest with Blomqvist coming second and George Plsek / Jeff Burmeister third. The second stage was won by Plsek; then Blomqvist won the next two. The final stage of the evening had to be cancelled as the organizers ran out of time in the gloom of the Portland evening. So by the end of day one, Plsek was leading from Blomqvist with Travis Pastrana / Christian Edstrom in third place.

For day two the weather changed and the rains came as the competition moved to the west for a series of stages around the Tillamook State Forest.

The first stage of the day went to Pastrana who beat Wyeth Gubelman / Cindy Krolikowski by two seconds. Matt Iorio / Ole Holter came third a further three seconds behind. The next stage, Bark Shanty, saw Blomqvist take the win over Pat Richard / Nathalie Richard; who came back to win the next two stages.

By the end of the first run through the forest, Blomqvist was leading with Pastrana second and Richard third. Plsek / Burmeister had retired with an electrical failure.

On the second run, Richard took fastest on the first stage by twelve seconds over Blomqvist—making three in a row and lifting him to second place. Then disaster struck when his gearbox failed halfway through Bark Shanty 2. His retirement left the fight for the lead to Blomqvist and Pastrana. By the end of the day, Blomqvist was leading Pastrana by forty seconds with Carl Jardevall / Amity Trowbridge third and Ken Block / Alex Gelsomino lying fourth.

Sunday started threatening rain but the skies cleared and the conditions ended up being perfect for the last five stages of the event. These were held further north around the town of Vernonia. Although

Center: Stig Blomqvist / Ana Goni with brakes aglow.

Bottom: Todd Lengacher / Les Green (Audi) at the raceway.

Matt Iorio / Ole Holter waiting to go.

Ken Block / Alex Gelsomino clip a hay bale.

Pastrana worked hard to keep the pressure on him, Blomqvist dominated the day—winning all five stages and increasing his lead to a winning margin of over one minute.

So, after nineteen stages, Blomqvist / Goni took the overall and Group N win and with a total time of 2:24:05, beating Pastrana / Edstrom with a time of 2:25:21. Third came Jardevall / Trowbridge who were a further ninety seconds behind Pastrana. They also won the Open Class. In fourth, Iorio / Holter managed to pull ahead of Gubelman / Krolikowski. Norman LeBlanc / Keith Morison took the PGT Class ahead of Foust / Crouch; while Mark Tabor / Kevin Poirier took the Production Class over Sans Thompson / Craig Marr.

After two events, Iorio was leading the championship but with Richard and Blomqvist both having only one scoring event each it was clear there was all to play for in Pennsylvania.

Mark Tabor / Kevin Poirier (Acura)
at the start of the Super Special.

Left: Carl Jardevall / Amity Trowbridge take a short-cut.

Below, left: Stig Blomqvist and David Sutton discuss strategy at Service.

Below, right: Travis Pastrana is ready for the restart from Service.

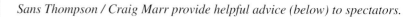

Sans Thompson / Craig Marr provide helpful advice (below) to spectators.

Travis Pastrana / Christian Edstrom would collect second overall.

Opposite, above: Fintan McCarthy / Matthew Collins spin out on the Super Special.

Opposite, below: Pat Richard / Nathalie Richard surrounded by media when they retire.

Lou Beck / Randee Hahn in their Toyota MR2.

Robert Olson / Ryan Johnson trying to order 20 more horsepower at service.

Oregon Trail Rally Schedule

Stage #	First Car	Stage Name	Miles
Friday, April 22			
1	5:00	Rally Start	
1	16:21	Armco Trail 1	1.84
2	16:44	Northwest Passage 1	1.92
3	17:07	Armco Trail 2	1.84
4	17:25	Northwest Passage 2	1.92
5	19:03	PIR Land Rush	4.00
Saturday, April 23			
6	11:33	On the Lookout	5.00
	11:52	Service	
7	12:35	Bark Shanty 1	10.90
8	13:08	Murphy Camp 1	7.26
9	13:36	East to South 1	6.99
	14:03	Service	
10	14:56	Bobcat 1	6.40
	15:17	Service	
11	16:00	Bark Shanty 2	10.90
12	16:33	Murphy Camp 2	7.26
13	17:01	East to South 2	6.99
	17:28	Service	
14	18:21	Bobcat 2	4.87
Sunday, April 24			
15	9:53	South Louie 1	10.03
16	10:24	Scotty's Jig 1	9.71
		Service	
17	12:43	Emerald Forest	9.51
		Service	
18	14:27	South Louie 2	10.03
19	15:01	Scotty's Jig 2	9.71
	15:59	Rally Finish	

Oregon Trail Rally Results

POSITION O'all	POSITION Class	Class	Car #	Driver Co-Driver	Car	SS-1	SS-2	SS-3	SS-4	SS-6	SS-7	SS-8	SS-9	SS-10	SS-11	SS-12	SS-13	SS-14	SS-15	SS-16	SS-17	SS-18	SS-19	Road Penalties	Total
1	1	GN	65	Stig Blomqvist / Ana Goni	Subaru STi WRX	01:32	02:16	01:35	02:09	05:27	13:39	08:25	09:02	07:29	13:42	08:27	09:09	06:07	11:20	11:16	10:16	11:15	10:59		2:24:05.3
2	2	GN	199	Travis Pastrana / Christian Edstrom	Subaru WRX STi	01:36	02:14	01:39	02:10	05:17	14:00	08:25	09:13	07:34	13:50	08:23	09:11	06:07	11:36	11:23	10:21	11:16	11:06		2:25:21.6
3	1	O	39	Carl Jardevall / Amity Trowbridge	Mitsubishi Evo	01:33	02:19	01:35	02:12	05:28	13:56	08:23	09:24	07:42	14:02	08:31	09:16	06:06	11:42	11:43	10:34	11:21	11:04		2:26:51.0
4	2	O	99	Matt Iorio / Ole Holter	Subaru Impreza	01:33	02:30	01:39	02:14	05:22	14:40	08:47	09:32	07:30	14:20	08:47	09:20	06:10	11:40	11:32	10:40	11:39	11:30		2:30:04.6
5	3	GN	103	Wyeth Gubelmann / Cindy Krolikowski	Subaru Impreza	01:34	02:23	01:36	02:17	05:19	14:15	08:57	09:50	07:49	14:17	08:51	09:39	06:19	12:19	11:58	10:45	11:49	11:42		2:31:39.3
6	4	GN	947	William Bacon / Peter Watt	Subaru Impreza	01:35	02:21	01:37	02:14	05:29	14:07	11:17	10:02	08:10	14:01	08:26	09:16	05:55	11:44	11:35	10:35	11:13	11:11	02:00.0	2:32:47.5
7	1	PGT	616	Norman LeBlanc / Keith Morison	Subaru Impreza WRX	01:38	02:22	01:44	02:16	05:40	14:38	08:51	09:51	08:47	14:46	08:54	09:38	06:19	12:01	11:44	11:06	11:48	11:35		2:33:39.6
8	5	GN	774	Otis Dimiters / Peter Monin	Subaru WRX STi	01:33	02:23	01:37	02:13	05:41	14:55	09:03	10:08	08:17	14:51	09:00	09:55	06:18	11:53	12:03	10:38	11:52	11:34		2:33:54.3
9	2	PGT	429	Tanner Foust / Scott Crouch	Subaru WRX	01:31	02:23	01:37	02:15	05:39	14:44	09:02	09:58	08:09	14:59	09:03	10:15	06:40	12:12	12:00	10:53	11:49	11:50		2:34:59.2
10	3	PGT	46	Matthew Johnson / Wendy Nakamoto	Subaru WRX	01:39	02:28	01:40	02:14	05:40	14:56	09:09	10:09	08:06	15:07	09:21	10:11	06:20	12:28	12:08	11:04	12:08	11:45	48	2:37:20.7
11	6	GN	676	Mark McElduff / Damien Irwin	Subaru WRX Sti	01:40	02:28	01:44	02:21	05:54	14:50	08:58	10:14	08:16	14:58	09:02	10:06	06:37	12:52	12:19	11:07	12:22	11:52		2:37:41.3
12	4	PGT	153	Eric Langbein / Jeremy Wimpey	Toyota Celica	01:37	02:47	01:42	02:29	05:57	15:28	09:14	10:49	08:20	15:22	09:14	10:06	06:45	12:37	13:00	11:20	12:05	11:48		2:40:41.6
13	3	O	288	Gary Cavett / John Dillon	Subaru Impreza	01:33	02:24	01:39	02:18	05:53	14:43	09:05	10:05	08:37	15:13	09:13	10:01	06:31	12:24	12:14	10:59	13:04	17:12		2:43:07.1
14	4	O	252	Bob Trinder / Adam Trinder	Subaru WRX	01:33	02:40	01:38	02:23	05:59	15:41	09:41	10:36	08:32	15:39	09:39	10:26	06:55	13:00	12:38	11:32	13:04	12:02		2:43:38.6
15	5	O	227	Derik Nelson / John Allen	Mitsubishi Evo 8	01:43	02:30	01:44	02:23	06:18	16:01	09:42	10:29	08:36	16:01	09:54	10:51	06:59	12:43	12:26	11:28	12:27	12:15		2:44:31.2
16	7	GN	43	Ken Block / Alex Gelsomino	Subaru WRX Sti	01:38	02:18	01:40	02:11	05:29	14:09	08:37	09:20	07:42	14:21	08:51	09:40	06:15	11:38	26:29	10:52	11:39	11:44	01:36.0	2:46:09.4
17	1	P	232	Mark Tabor / Kevin Poirier	Acura RSX Type S	01:46	02:38	01:50	02:32	06:15	16:28	10:07	11:12	09:24	16:51	10:38	11:39	07:17	13:47	13:28	12:22	13:04	12:45		2:54:04.6
18	6	O	558	Jim Cox / Tim Sardelich	Chevrolet S10	01:41	02:30	01:52	02:35	06:33	17:13	10:23	11:25	09:22	16:39	10:32	11:32	07:29	13:36	13:05	12:52	13:04	13:53		2:56:15.7
19	2	P	49	Sans Thompson / Craig Marr	Dodge Neon	01:44	02:40	01:47	02:48	06:42	17:10	10:26	11:59	09:41	17:19	10:15	11:52	07:39	14:43	13:47	12:42	13:04	13:41	12	3:00:09.0
20	7	O	14	Amy BeberVanzo / Claire Chizma	Mitsubishi Evo 8	01:52	02:50	01:59	02:41	06:35	17:08	10:38	12:12	09:42	17:42	11:03	12:08	07:52	13:47	13:41	12:35	13:04	13:29		3:00:58.2
21	3	P	231	April Smith / Jeff Zurschmeide	Geo Metro	02:11	03:18	02:14	03:01	07:23	20:29	11:43	13:12	11:26	21:22	12:30	13:51	09:41	16:33	15:31	13:19	13:04	14:44		3:25:32.2
		PGT	215	Jamie Thomas / Matt Gauger	Subaru WRX Wagon	01:40	02:27	01:45	02:21	05:45	15:10	09:02	10:02	08:15	15:06	09:09	10:02	06:34	12:30	11:53	10:57				DNF
		PGT	866	Timothy Penasack / Rob McLelland	Subaru WRX	01:40	02:38	01:44	02:28	06:23	15:58	09:28	10:41	08:46	15:51	09:34	10:39	07:43	13:06	56:09					DNF
		G2	292	Derek Bottles / Jason Grahn	VW Golf	01:43	02:31	01:46	02:29	06:02	15:27	09:12	10:16	08:31	15:26	09:26									DNF
		GN	1	Pat Richard / Nathalie Richard	Subaru WRX	01:54	02:19	01:39	02:14	05:29	13:50	08:19	08:59	07:17											DNF
		O	207	Dave Hintz / Rick Hintz	Subaru WRX	01:35	02:35	01:39	02:19	05:44	15:07	09:15	09:58	08:11											DNF
		GN	600	Fintan McCarthy / Matthews Collins	Subaru WRX STi	01:44	02:50	01:45	02:35	06:08	15:18	09:01	10:05	08:15											DNF
		G5	60	Bruce Davis / Jimmy Brandt	Dodge SRT4	01:37	02:34	01:41	02:25	06:24	16:31	10:14	11:26	08:59											DNF
		PGT	323	Stephan Verdier / Allan Walker	Subaru WRX	01:34	02:20	01:35	02:15	05:26	14:16	09:45													DNF
		O	30	George Plsek / Jeff Burmeister	Mitsubishi Evo	01:32	02:08	01:37	02:14	05:55	16:44														DNF

Stig Blomqvist / Ana Goni take the win.

Pat Richard / Nathalie Richard are the winners. Photo courtesy of Lorne Trezise.

SUBARU
RIM OF THE WORLD

Lancaster, California

May 6–7, 2005

It was the weather that dominated the twenty-second running of the Subaru Rim of the World. Southern California had suffered heavy rainfall for some time leading up to the event. Many of the roads were waterlogged and the organizers were forced to eliminate some of the traditional stages. For example, the Saturday morning North Boundary stages were impassable due to lying water and had to be cut. Even the first run through the Antelope Valley Fairgrounds spectator stage had to be demoted to a demonstration run.

Defending their win from last year, Pat Richard / Nathalie Richard were favorites. But they were expected to have close competition from Leon Styles / Mark McAllister, and Peter Workum / Chrissie Beavis. All three teams had entered Subarus. U.S. Championship leader Tom Lawless was not entered.

Styles was the first to have problems when he had to retire on the way from service to the stadium when a bearing seized.

Left: Matt Iorio / Ole Holter take second place.
Photo courtesy of Lorne Trezise.

Wyeth Gubelmann / Cindy Krolikowski.
Photo courtesy of Lorne Trezise.

The Friday evening provided two stages—a double running of the Del Sur stage. As the competitors returned to their hotels, Richard was in first place, followed forty-four seconds behind by Matt Iorio / Ole Holter, then Ken Block / Alex Gelsomino a further three seconds behind. First of the top seeds to be claimed by the Angeles Forests were Wyeth Gubelman / Cindy Krolikowski who went off the course on the first pass of Del Sur.

The Saturday schedule had to be a work-in-progress throughout the day as the organizers worked to respond to the challenges of the water-soaked conditions. The first stage to run was Powerline that was won by Block followed by Workum and Iorio. The second pass was won by Richard—a full twenty-three seconds ahead of Iorio, then Block.

Pat Richard / Nathalie Richard.
Photo courtesy of Lorne Trezise.

After running the Super Special stage the teams went back into the forests for two passes of the Magic Mountain and Messenger Flats stages. By the time they returned to the fairgrounds, Richard had consolidated a three-minute lead over Iorio, then Block.

After two further passes on the Del Sur stages, the event concluded with a final timed run of the Super Special stage at the fairgrounds. Workum crashed out without injury but the top three places did not change. Pat Richard / Nathalie Richard won the event by a clear five minutes followed by Matt Iorio / Ole Holter and Ken Block / Alex Gelsomino.

After two rounds of the series, the leader was Iorio—having scored in both rounds. Lawless and Richard were joint second.

Matt Johnson / Wendy Nakamoto.
Photo courtesy of Lorne Trezise.

Dennis Martin / Kim DeMotte.
Photo courtesy of Lorne Trezise.

The Bill Malik / Amity Trowbridge
Volvo kicks the dirt.
Photo courtesy of Lorne Trezise.

Ken Block / Alex Gelsomino.
Photo courtesy of Lorne Trezise.

The Subaru of Victor Kuhns / Abel
Villesca needs help to be pulled
from the shrubbery.
Photo courtesy of Lorne Trezise.

Jim Pierce / Amar Sehmi.
Photo courtesy of Lorne Trezise.

Jeff Rados / Jeff Dubrule in their Ford Ranger. Photo courtesy of Lorne Trezise.

George Plsek / Jeff Burmeister in their Mitsubishi. Photo courtesy of Lorne Trezise.

Brooks Freehill / Brian McGuire in the Thule VW. Photo courtesy of Lorne Trezise.

Subaru Rim of the World Rally Schedule

Stage #	First Car	Stage Name	Miles
Friday, May 6			
	19:00	Rally Start	
1	19:17	Antelope Valley Fairground	0.7
2	20:05	Del Sur South	7.6
3	21:30	Del Sur North	7.6
Saturday, May 7			
4	8:28	Power Line 1	15.3
5	8:51	North Boundary 1	3.1
6	9:44	Powerline 2	5.3
7	10:08	North Boundary 2	3.1
		Service	
8	12:00	Antelope Valley Fairground	0.7
9	13:09	Magic Mountain East	8.7
10	13:33	Messenger Flats East	8.9
11	15:07	Messenger Flats West	8.9
12	15:34	Magic Mountain West	8.7
		Service	
13	17:35	Antelope Valley Fairground	0.7
14	18:24	Del Sur South	7.8
15	19:41	Del Sur North	7.8
		Service	
16	20:58	Antelope Valley Fairground	0.7
		Rally Finish	

Ole Holter and Matt Iorio wait for the action.
Photo courtesy of Matthew Simmons.

Subaru Rim of the World Rally Results

POSITION O'all	POSITION Class	Class	Car #	Driver	Co-Driver	Car	SS-1	SS-2	SS-3	SS-4	SS-6	SS-9	SS-10	SS-11	SS-12	SS-13	SS-14	SS-15	Road Penalties	Total
1	1	O4	1	Pat Richard	Nathalie Richard	Subaru WRX		9.85	10.15	8.68	8.36	10.22	14.15	12.34	10.65	2.24	9.86	10.04		106.54
2	2	O4	99	Matt Iorio	Ole Holter	Subaru Impreza STi		10.24	10.49	8.67	8.59	10.42	14.36	14.26	11.01	2.39	10.48	10.72		111.63
3	1	GN	43	Ken Block	Alex Gelsomino	Subaru WRX STi		10.24	10.54	8.63	8.65	10.60	14.50	14.65	11.42	2.21	10.50	11.09		113.03
4	1	SS	323	Stephan Verdier	Allan Walker	Subaru WRX		10.44	10.89	8.75	8.82	10.42	14.96	15.03	11.20	2.32	11.07	11.33		115.23
5	2	SS	46	Matt Johnson	Wendy Nakamoto	Subaru WRX		10.69	10.90	9.36	9.08	10.75	14.93	15.59	11.22	2.28	10.49	10.94		116.23
6	2	GN	22	Ralph Kosmides	Jimmy Brandt	Subaru Impreza		10.91	10.95	9.56	9.10	11.00	14.88	15.33	11.75	2.40	10.84	11.23		117.95
7	3	O4	989	Erik Lyden	Jay Socha	Subaru Legacy		11.22	11.39	9.65	9.52	11.02	14.96	16.32	11.96	2.50	11.28	11.34		121.16
8	1	O2	28	Bill Malik	Amity Trowbridge	Volvo		12.71	12.12	9.81	9.60	11.36	14.96	16.13	12.24	2.54	11.73	11.67		124.87
9	2	O2	60	Bruce Davis	Lee Sorenson	Dodge Neon SRT-4		12.21	12.11	9.92	10.62	11.03	16.61	15.73	11.52	2.60	11.75	11.91		126.01
10	3	O2	290	Craig Hollingsworth	Jason Grahn	VW Jetta GLi		11.19	11.12	9.79	9.73	11.70	14.96	18.39	13.07	2.55	11.86	11.97	0.20	126.53
11	4	O2	418	Jimmy Keeney	Brian Moody	Honda Civic		11.79	12.62	9.79	10.72	12.27	16.49	16.14	11.89	2.72	12.42	12.45		129.30
12	3	SS	368	Marvin Ronquillo	John Burke	Subaru WRX		12.30	12.80	12.24	15.73	12.17	17.78	17.09	12.63	2.45	13.43	13.62		142.24
		O4	6	Peter Workum	Chrissie Beavis	Subaru WRX		10.43	10.69	8.64	8.67	11.93	14.96	15.12	11.18	2.57	10.61			
		GN	103	Wyeth Gubelmann	Cindy Krolikowski	Subaru WRX STi		76.45	18.83	9.19	8.85	10.50	14.36	15.70	11.07	2.36	10.44	10.84		
		O2	122	Dennis Martin	Kim DeMotte	Ford Focus		12.68	12.66	9.84	9.78	11.79	16.11	15.91	12.17					
		O4	30	George Plsek	Jeff Burmeister	Mitsubishi Lancer Evo		10.81	11.10	9.00	8.78	10.52	14.29	14.61						
		O4	558	Jim Pierce	Amar Sehmi	Chevrolet S10		11.12	11.30	9.24	9.37	11.16								
		GN	89	Wolfgang Hoeck	John Dillon	Mitsubishi Lancer Evo VII		10.60	10.90	8.88										
		O2	776	Lisa Klassen	Casey Blust	Toyota Corolla		12.86	13.64	11.70										
		O4	374	Leon Styles	Mark McAllister	Mitsubishi Lancer Evo VII		0.00	0.00											
		GN	423	Victor Kuhns	Abel Villesca	Subaru WRX STi		10.70	10.87										1.20	
		O4	127	Chad Dykes	Brian Coats	Chevrolet S10		10.56	12.39										3.20	
		O2	96	Brian Scott	David Hackett	Ford Focus SVT		11.23	11.67											
		O2	407	Brooks Freehill	Brian McGuire	VW Jetta		11.71	11.96	9.70	26.27	11.49	14.96	21.11	27.90	2.41			0.20	

The Porsche of Dennis Chizma.
Photo courtesy of Lorne Trezise.

Pat Richard / Nathalie Richard take to the water.

STPR2005

SUSQUEHANNOCK TRAIL PRO RALLY

Wellsboro, Pennsylvania

June 4, 2005

Enda McCormack / Mark McAllister get air.

The championship contenders had to cross the country again for the third round of the Rally America series; this time to Wellsboro, Pennsylvania for the twenty-ninth running of the Susquehannock Trail ProRally—affectionately know as the STPR. It's a single-day event, starting in the morning and running until nearly midnight. After some rain during the practice day, the race day was dry and comfortable—in the high sixties.

Going into the event, the championship leaders were Matt Iorio / Ole Holter. Stig Blomqvist / Pauline Gullick and Pat Richard / Nathalie Richard were also entered and their duel was expected to be the highlight of the event. Though they were both competing in Group N cars which were at a disadvantage to the power of the Open class cars on this smooth and fast event. The favorites to win the event were Paul Choiniere / Jeff Becker in their Open class Hyundai Tiburon.

The first stage of the morning was the spectator's favorite—Subaru Splash. This fast and smooth six-mile stage ends in the middle of a ford crossing a river. As usual, the well-practiced fire team had to pull several competitors out of the water when their engines died. First on the road, Matt Iorio / Ole Holter avoided that fate but did damage their car when they dove into the water at full

Chris Gilligan / Joe Peterson have a suspension failure before hitting the water . . .

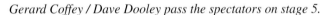

Gerard Coffey / Dave Dooley pass the spectators on stage 5.

speed. Choiniere posted fastest time at 5:17 and went on to score fastest times on the next two stages.

By the end of the morning session, four stages had been run and Choiniere was leading the Subaru of Shane Mitchell / Glenn Paterson by thirteen seconds. In third place were Travis Pastrana / Christian Edstrom. Blomqvist and Richard were still in contention along with Tom Lawless / Jason Gillespie in their Mitsubishi Evo.

The first stage out on the evening run was Lee Stock. At twenty-one miles this is the longest stage of the event. Mitchell scored fastest time on the stage at 18:49. Just five seconds behind was Choiniere followed by Blomqvist, Pastrana and Richard.

Stage 6, Lee Buck Randall, saw Mitchell score over Choiniere again—this time by thirteen seconds. But then Choiniere got a second wind to collect the next two stages.

Final stage honors went to Richard who blasted the last stage some fourteen seconds ahead of Lawless— enough to let him steal fourth place.

At the end of the event the win went to Paul Choiniere / Jeff Becker in a Hyundai Tiburon. This was Choiniere's ninth win at the event. He was followed by

. . . and need help from the rescue team.

*Travis Pastrana / Christian Edstrom
were in contention until stage 7.*

Irishmen Shane Mitchell / Glenn Paterson in their Subaru then the Group N Subarus of Blomqvist / Gullick and Richard / Richard coming third and fourth.

By the end of STPR, we had had three events and three winners; and there were only four points separating the top three competitors for the championship. The points gap was inevitably going to widen at the Pikes Peak.

Shane Mitchell / Glenn Patterson climb
out of the water splash.

Pat Richard / Nathalie Richard
with front brakes aglow.

Tim Penasack / Marc Goldfarb come in second in PGT Class.

Below: Eric Langbein / Jeremy Wimpey place first in PGT.

Jonathan Bottoms / Carolyn Bosley are ninth overall.

Jim Cox / Joshua Bressen cross the finish line on stage 1.

Below: Matt Johnston / Alex Kihurani entertain the crowd at the hairpin on stage 3.

Ken Block / Alex Gelsomino are bemused to find themselves in the marshland during practice.

Susquehannock Trail Pro Rally Schedule

Stage #	First Car	Stage Name	Miles
Saturday, June 4			
	10:31	Rally Start	
1	10:56	Subaru Splash	6.05
		Service - Stony Fork	
2	12:08	Asaph Run	10.05
3	12:50	Thompson Point	10.99
4	13:15	Sliders Francis	11.24
		Service - Morris	
5	17:31	Lee Stock 1	21.27
6	18:05	Lee Buck Randall 1	13.09
7	18:39	Lebo Mile 1	10.36
		Service - Germania	
8	21:08	Lee Stock 2	21.27
9	21:42	Lee Buck Randall 2	13.09
10	22:16	Lebo Mile 2	10.36
		Service - Germania	
	23:38	Rally Finish	

Otis Dimiters / Peter Monin win the prize for the highest splash!

Wojciech Okula / Adam Pelc.

Susquehannock Trail Pro Rally (STPR) Results

POSITION O'all	Class	Class	Car #	Driver	Co-Driver	Car	SS-1	SS-2	SS-3	SS-4	SS-5	SS-6	SS-7	SS-8	SS-9	SS-10	Road Penalties	Total
1	1	O	11	Paul Choiniere	Jeff Becker	2003 Hyundai Tiburon	05:17.0	08:36.4	09:34.2	10:26.0	18:54.6	11:31.1	09:43.7	19:15.0	0	10:27.9		1:43:45.9
2	2	O	45	Shane Mitchell	Glenn Patterson	2000 Subaru Impreza	05:22.0	08:47.5	09:36.7	10:20.1	18:49.2	11:18.0	10:06.3	20:04.2	0	10:36.2		1:45:00.2
3	1	GN	65	Stig Blomqvist	Pauline Gullick	2003 Subaru Impreza	05:29.0	08:48.0	09:40.8	10:33.8	19:09.6	11:49.5	10:07.8	20:07.2	0	10:25.8		1:46:11.5
4	2	GN	1	Patrick Richard	Nathalie Richard	2002 Subaru Impreza WRX	05:43.0	09:07.0	09:53.7	10:27.7	19:23.4	11:57.2	10:07.8	19:52.2	0	10:01.5		1:46:33.5
5	3	O	116	Tom Lawless	Jason Gillespie	2003 Mitsubishi Evo 8	05:35.0	08:49.1	09:53.3	10:43.0	19:25.8	12:04.7	10:07.8	19:43.2	0	10:15.5		1:46:37.4
6	3	GN	43	Ken Block	Alessandro Gelsomino	2004 Subaru WRX	05:36.0	08:57.5	10:13.6	10:54.9	19:52.8	12:12.4	10:07.8	20:25.2	0	11:23.2		1:49:43.4
7	4	O	18	Matthew Iorio	Ole Holter	1997 Subaru Impreza	05:44.0	09:14.4	11:02.3	12:06.0	20:40.2	12:50.8	10:07.8	20:56.4	0	11:17.5		1:53:59.4
8	4	GN	774	Otis Dimiters	Peter Monin	2002 Subaru Impreza	05:46.0	09:20.5	10:00.4	13:39.0	20:07.8	12:25.0	10:07.8	20:37.8	0	12:11.6	12	1:54:27.9
9	5	GN	91	Jonathan Bottoms	Carolyn Bosley	2002 Subaru WRX	05:48.0	09:32.2	10:29.4	11:28.7	21:15.0	13:05.4	10:07.8	21:40.8	0	11:26.3		1:54:53.6
10	5	O	768	Celsus Donnelly	Barry McCann	2000 Mitsubishi Evo	05:49.0	09:50.3	10:44.6	11:57.7	20:30.0	13:03.3	10:07.8	21:48.0	0	11:50.9		1:55:41.6
11	6	O	874	Daniel O'Brien	Stephen Duffy	2005 Subaru WRX	05:57.0	09:51.5	10:45.8	11:48.0	21:29.4	13:04.4	10:07.8	21:36.0	0	11:31.1		1:56:11.0
12	7	O	977	Martin Donnelly	Chrissie Beavis	1997 Mitsubishi Evo IV	06:03.0	09:42.9	10:30.4	11:36.4	21:25.2	13:00.9	10:07.8	21:56.4	0	11:50.7		1:56:13.7
13	8	O	902	Enda McCormack	Mark McAllister	2001 Mitsubishi Evo VI	06:10.0	10:11.7	11:05.2	11:27.4	21:03.6	12:55.9	10:07.8	22:06.6	0	12:19.2		1:57:27.4
14	9	O	868	Gerard Coffey	Dave Dooley	2004 Mitsubishi Evo 8	05:17.0	10:15.4	10:54.8	11:59.5	21:43.2	13:10.0	10:07.8	22:15.6	0	11:52.1		1:57:35.4
15	10	O	93	Bob Olson	Ryan Johnson	1999 Subaru RS	06:03.0	09:54.6	11:01.6	11:48.9	21:43.2	13:22.5	10:07.8	23:19.2	0	12:07.0		1:59:27.8
16	6	GN	44	Henry Krolikowski	Cindy Krolikowski	2000 Subaru WRX	06:24.0	10:16.1	11:14.5	12:13.8	21:34.8	13:21.2	10:07.8	22:43.2	0	11:45.1		1:59:40.5
17	1	PGT	153	Eric Langbein	Jeremy Wimpey	1988 Toyota Celica	06:04.0	09:56.2	10:58.1	14:37.0	21:20.4	13:09.8	10:07.8	21:42.6	0	11:20.7	36	1:59:52.6
18	2	PGT	866	Tim Penasack	Marc Goldfarb	2002 Subaru Impreza	06:19.0	10:11.2	11:37.3	12:10.0	22:03.0	13:41.2	10:07.8	22:49.8	0	11:52.4		2:00:51.7
19	3	PGT	429	Tanner Foust	Scott Crouch	2002 Subaru WRX	05:51.0	09:38.5	10:48.7	12:02.1	23:33.6	13:29.1	10:07.8	22:03.0	0	12:00.4	02:12.0	2:01:46.2
20	4	PGT	884	Tim Stevens	Jeff Hagan	2002 Subaru WRX	06:29.0	10:36.5	11:37.8	12:17.9	22:22.2	13:52.4	10:07.8	23:23.4	0	12:45.3		2:03:32.3
21	7	GN	199	Travis Pastrana	Christian Edstrom	2004 Subaru WRX	05:21.0	08:58.8	09:43.0	10:17.6	19:19.8	12:00.4	27:51.9	20:00.0	0	10:32.8		2:04:05.3
22	11	O	48	Cyril Kearney	Charlie Bradley	2005 Subaru WRX	06:30.0	10:26.1	11:10.7	12:21.5	23:44.4	14:40.8	10:07.8	25:24.0	0	13:09.3		2:07:34.6
23	12	O	508	Tom Ottey	Pamela McGarvery	1989 Mazda 323 GTX	06:00.0	09:52.6	10:47.3	11:37.4	22:36.0	17:36.6	10:07.8	29:04.8	0	13:52.4		2:11:34.9
24	1	G2	587	Matt Johnston	Alex Kihurani	1992 Honda Civic	07:11.0	11:33.2	12:30.7	13:02.0	24:52.8	14:59.9	10:07.8	26:14.4	0	14:04.7		2:14:36.5
25	2	G2	845	John Sundelin	J Duffy Bowers	2002 Ford Focus	07:28.0	11:31.1	12:51.5	13:42.0	24:57.6	16:00.9	10:07.8	27:07.8	0	13:56.1		2:17:42.8
26	13	O	558	Jim Cox	Joshua Bressen	2004 Chevrolet S10	07:12.0	12:34.8	12:53.0	13:46.4	25:36.6	15:29.0	10:07.8	26:53.4	0	14:34.4	04:00.0	2:23:07.4
		GN	964	David Anton	Andrew Coombs	2002 Subaru WRX	06:03.0	09:47.1	10:32.2	12:16.8	21:05.4	11:58.3	10:07.8	25:55.0				DNF
		O	173	Patrick Lilly	Noel Gallagher	1999 Mitsubishi Evo IV	06:08.0	09:35.8	10:51.0	11:52.0	21:10.8	12:57.0	10:07.8					DNF
		GN	676	Mark McElduff	Scott Putnam	2002 Subaru WRX	05:57.0	09:46.5	10:51.0	11:25.6	20:41.4							DNF
		O	907	Patrick Brennan	Domach OLeary	2004 Subaru WRX	05:59.0	09:42.7	11:02.7	11:41.4								DNF
		G5	143	Chris Whiteman	Mike Paulin	2004 Dodge SRT4	06:01.8	09:50.8	11:12.4									DNF
		O	769	Keith Kreisler	Steve McKelvie	1995 Subaru WRX	06:11.0											DNF
		O	27	Chris Gilligan	Joe Peterson	1997 Mitsubishi Evo IV	07:02.0											DNF
		GN	945	Brendan Kelly	Bob Kelly	2002 Subaru WRX												DNF
		G5	72	Jon Hamilton	Ken Sabo	2000 Volkswagen Golf TDI												DNF
		O	74	Ramana Lagemann	Mark Williams	1997 Ford Escort Cosworth												DNF

Paul Choiniere / Jeff Becker win the event.

Stephan Verdier / Chrissie Beavis win Pikes Peak.

FALKEN TIRE PIKES PEAK INTERNATIONAL HILL CLIMB

Colorado Springs, Colorado
June 22–25, 2005

Leon Styles / Theron Pace kick stones over the edge.

The most popular spectator point on Pikes Peak is the Devil's Playground. Even at a height of 12,780 feet it is not at the top of the mountain, but it offers a vantage point from which you can watch the competitors as they work their way through some of the 156 turns it takes to climb 4,800 feet to the 14,110 feet summit. This tortuous road is 12.442 miles long.

It's a tough event. Not only because the height affects car's performance but the road is a mix of asphalt and gravel with no guardrails and many vertical drops. It requires a bucketful of courage and a powerful car to win. There are really two events in one. For the entrants in the Falken Tire Pikes Peak International Hill Climb, there is a week of practicing and qualifying for a single timed run up the hill to determine the winner. For the rally entrants, the organizers have made a single-venue event with seven stages by using different parts of the hill on different days.

The weather held throughout the event. For morning runs, the temperature at the summit of the hill was a reasonable 40°F and could improve by up to 15° towards the base.

With the championship still wide open there were entries from all the major teams with the exception of

Jim Goertz leads a group of Quads.

Jeff Ewing power slides round Double Cut.

Matt Iorio. Stig Blomqvist / Ana Goni were entered in the David Sutton prepared Subaru; Pat Richard / Nathalie Richard in their Group N Subaru.

Stephan Verdier was driving the Autosport Engineering prepared Subaru usually driven by Peter Workum. He was co-driven by Chrissie Beavis, Workum's usual co-driver.

The first day, Wednesday, included three stages. The first stage was an all-asphalt climb to the Crystal Reservoir. Verdier took fastest time—five seconds ahead of Doug Shepherd / Chris Whiteman in their Dodge Neon SRT-4. Richard was third and Blomqvist fourth. The second stage took the competitors to the Picnic grounds. It went

Mike Ryan takes the hill in his Big Rig.

to Shepherd followed by Richard, then Blomqvist. When the teams returned to the reservoir to repeat the climb this time ending at Glen Clove it was Verdier who came back to take it from Shepherd and Blomqvist.

So, by the end of the first day, Verdier was leading with Shepherd second and Richard third.

After a day off, the teams returned on the Friday for another day of action. Stage 4 repeated Glen Cove and went to Shepherd then Verdier. Last year's victor Leon Styles was third, co-driven by Therin Pace. Then Verdier and Styles came in first and second on the next two stages—a double running of the gravel climb from Glen Cove to the Summit—so that the day ended with Verdier leading the rally some fifty seconds ahead of Richard, then Styles just 1.5 seconds behind.

The final day of the rally was run at the same time as the hill climb and, for the first time, the competitors used the whole hill as one stage. It was won by Verdier with a time of 12:17, some ten seconds ahead of Styles then Blomqvist.

Stephan Verdier / Chrissie Beavis won the event with an overall time of 42:08—more than a minute ahead of second place Leon Styles / Therin Pace. Third overall and first in Group N were Stig Blomqvist and Ana Goni.

Other class winners were Doug Shepherd / Chris Whiteman (Group 5), Tanner Foust / Scott Crouch (PGT) and Sans Thompson / Craig Marr (Production).

After four events, we had had four overall winners! So it had been car reliability and consistent driving that allowed Blomqvist to pull ahead in the championship.

Above: George Plsek / Jeff Burmeister at Double Cut.

Right: Bob Wall / Robert Gray make the crest at the Devil's Playground.

Doug Shepherd / Chris Whiteman use all the road.

Bobby Regester is disconsolate after his Pontiac-based Super Stock fails.

*Travis Pastrana /
Christian Edstrom place
third in Group N.*

A selection of images from the Hill Climb.

Doug Havir / Scott Putnam kick dust on their way to Devil's Playground.

Matt Johnson / Wendy Nakamoto zip through the ski area.

Doug Shepherd / ChrisWhiteman take second overall.

A spectator watches as Tanner Foust / Scott Crouch climb the hill.

Pikes Peak International Hill Climb Schedule

Stage #	FirstCar	Stage Name	Miles
Wednesday, June 22			
		Rally Start	
1	19:03	Crystal Reservoir	4.80
2	19:18	Picnic	2.43
3	20:12	Glen Cove 1	5.49
Friday, June 24			
4	5:30	Glen Cove 2	5.49
5	5:47	Summit 1	6.05
6	6:58	Summit 2	6.05
Saturday, June 25			
7	9:45	Hill Climb	12.23
		Rally Finish	

Mark Utecht / Rob Bohn in their Subaru.

Falken Tire Pikes Peak International Hill Climb Results

POSITION O'all	POSITION Class	Class	Car #	Driver Co-Driver	Car	SS-1	SS-2	SS-3	SS-4	SS-5	SS-6	SS-7	Road Penalties	Total
1	1	O	124	Stephan Verdier / Chrissie Beavis	2002 Subaru WRX	03:43.0	02:22.5	05:31.7	05:30.3	06:26.4	06:17.3	12:17.6		42:08.8
2	2	O	374	Leon Styles / Therin Pace	2000 Mitsubishi Evo 7	04:06.0	02:22.5	05:42.4	05:32.2	06:30.0	06:30.4	12:27.6		43:11.1
3	1	GN	65	Stig Blomqvist / Ana Goni	2003 Subaru WRX	03:53.0	02:13.9	05:41.1	05:37.8	06:44.6	06:41.2	12:32.3		43:23.9
4	2	GN	1	Patrick Richard / Nathalie Richard	2004 Subaru WRX	03:49.0	02:12.4	05:46.5	05:38.0	06:36.7	06:39.4	12:42.5		43:24.5
5	3	O	88	Doug Havir / Scott Putnam	2004 Subaru WRX STi	04:01.0	02:18.9	05:51.7	05:37.8	06:37.3	06:36.1	12:41.5		43:44.3
6	1	G5	52	Doug Shepherd / Chris Whiteman	2004 Dodge STR-4	03:48.0	02:10.2	05:40.7	05:28.7	07:55.8	06:32.3	12:37.2		44:12.9
7	3	GN	199	Travis Pastrana / Christian Edstrom	2004 Subaru WRX STi	04:03.0	02:20.1	05:51.1	05:49.3	06:54.7	06:46.1	12:58.9		44:43.2
8	4	O	30	George Plsek / Jeff Burmeister	2000 Mitsubishi Evo	04:06.0	02:22.5	06:01.6	05:42.6	06:55.6	07:02.7	12:49.5		45:00.5
9	1	PGT	429	Tanner Foust / Scott Crouch	2002 Subaru WRX	04:10.0	02:22.5	06:05.4	05:56.2	07:08.7	06:59.7	13:05.4		45:47.9
10	4	GN	43	Ken Block / Alex Gelsimino	2004 Subaru WRX STi	04:05.0	02:20.9	06:00.9	05:57.3	07:07.1	07:00.6	13:19.1		45:50.9
11	5	O	73	Michael Whitman / Bill Westrick	1995 Ford Escort	04:13.0	02:22.5	06:04.8	05:52.8	07:07.9	07:23.3	13:07.5		46:11.8
12	5	GN	83	Mark Utecht / Rob Bohn	2004 Subaru WRX	04:07.0	02:19.4	06:03.9	05:55.0	07:15.9	07:07.5	13:34.2		46:22.9
13	2	PGT	46	Matt Johnson / Wendy Nakamoto	2000 Subaru WRX	04:13.0	02:22.5	06:23.5	06:07.5	07:17.3	07:14.9	13:37.4	01:00.0	48:16.1
14	3	PGT	153	Eric Langbein / Jeremy Wimpey	1988 Toyota Celica Alltrac	04:28.0	02:22.5	06:28.7	06:19.6	07:55.2	07:42.0	14:20.1		49:36.1
15	4	PGT	821	Bob Wall / Robert Gray	2002 Subaru WRX	04:29.0	02:22.5	06:36.2	06:21.1	08:04.9	07:44.8	14:25.9		50:04.4
16	6	O	558	Jim Cox / Rebecca Greek	2004 Chevy S10	04:47.0	02:22.5	06:40.8	06:39.4	07:43.8	07:52.0	14:22.5		50:28.0
17	2	G5	432	Ron Nelson / Sara Malsom	1992 Eagle Talon	04:17.0	02:22.5	06:19.6	06:17.1	07:31.9	10:34.3	14:12.6	01:00.0	52:35.0
18	1	P	49	Sans Thompson / Craig Marr	2001 Dodge Neon	04:48.0	02:22.5	07:02.7	06:43.8	08:35.4	08:18.8	15:31.2		53:22.4
19	2	P	550	Dennis Sletten / Jonathon Stiles	1992 Jeep Cherokee	05:41.0	02:22.5	07:53.2	07:33.3	09:19.6	09:09.3	16:49.1		58:48.0
20	3	P	725	Dave Carapetyan / Ryan Schnell	1998 Acura Integra	04:47.0	02:22.5	07:21.7	06:54.7	08:27.1	08:15.5	15:40.2	05:00.0	58:48.7
		O	13	J.B. Niday / Dave Kean	1997 Subaru Impreza				06:36.3	0	09:52.6			DNF
		G5	443	Ryan Oerter / Karen Tracy	1985 Mazda RX7	0			06:50.5	08:50.0	08:11.4			DNF
		GN	103	Wyeth Gubelman / Cynthia Krolikowski	2004 Subaru WRX	03:57.0			06:02.2	07:16.9	07:01.3			DNF
		G5	42	Eric Burmeister / Dave Shindle	2005 Mazda 3	04:19.0	02:22.5	06:17.4	06:39.8	0				DNF
		G5	60	Bruce Davis / Jimmy Brandt	2000 Dodge SRT-4	04:25.0	02:22.5	06:28.6	06:19.0	07:49.8				DNF

Stig Blomqvist / Ana Goni take Group N.

Ramana Lagemann / Michael Fennell in their Escort on stage 1.

Nathalie Richard checks the Roadbook.

Ken Block / Alex Gelsomino dig the dust.

Left: Stig Blomqvist / Ana Goni are second overall.

first day—the high flying Concord Pond—claimed Pastrana who spun off the road damaging his Subaru sufficiently enough that he could not continue.

So, at the end of day one, Chomiere led from Richard with a consistent drive from Ken Block / Alex Gelsomino putting them in third place.

For the second day, the competitors would travel further afield to the stages around Oquossoc then dip into New Hampshire for the final stages in the Berlin area. Blomqvist took stage 5—Middle Dam—by seven seconds from Richard. Doug Havir / Scott Putman were third fastest.

The second running of Middle Dam was won by Blomqvist; with second place shared by Havir and Otis Dimiters / Alan Ockwell.

When the teams entered New Hampshire Richard reasserted himself taking stage 7—Dillon Success— by eleven seconds from Blomqvist. Stage 8— Marigrande—was taken by Gerard Coffey / Dave

Gerard Coffey / Dave Dooley entertain the crowd on stage 6.

Below: Doug Havir / Scott Putnam would run a great event until hitting a rock on stage 7.

Matt Iorio at Parc Exposé.

Matt Johnson / Wendy Nakamoto take the Production GT class.

Dooley with Blomqvist ahead of Richard; but it was Richard who came back to win the final stage and thus the event.

Pat Richard / Nathalie Richard took maximum points over Stig Blomqvist / Ana Goni with Ken Block / Alex Gelsomino in third place. His second championship win would put Richard ahead in the race for the drivers title, but there was still plenty of racing to come.

Andrew Comrie-Picard times Matt Johnson / Wendy Nakamoto.

Travis Pastrana / Christian Edstrom would crash out on stage 4.

Pat Richard waits for the start.

Niall Smith / Damen Treanor in their Mitsubishi.

Travis Pastrana takes a protein break.

Spectators play ball as they wait for the start of the stage.

John Cassidy/Dave Getchell fly their Subaru.

Maine Forest Rally Schedule

Stage #	First Car	Stage Name	Miles
Friday, July 29			
	14:30	Rally Start	
1	14:43	Mexico Rec.	0.50
2	15:36	South Arm	10.50
		Service - Oquossoc	
3	17:31	Bemis Mountain	10.50
		Service - Mexico	
4	19:33	Concord Pond	5.60
Saturday, July 30			
5	10:38	Middle Dam In	13.80
6	12:30	Middle Dam Out	15.50
		Service - Errol	
7	15:28	Dillon Success 1	12.20
8	16:05	Marigrande Road	6.20
9	16:40	Dillon Success 2	12.20
	17:51	Rally Finish	

Above: Stig Blomqvist waits for the start.

Right: Dave Anton / Andrew Coombs at the Spectator Area on stage 7.

Travis Pastrana / Christian Edstrom on stage 1.

OJIBWE FORESTS RALLY

Bemidji, Minnesota
August 26–27, 2005

The sixth round of the Rally America series took to the forests again. This time in the north of Minnesota—centered in Bemidji. It's a two-day event starting on Friday evening in the Paul Bunyan State Forest; then moving to the area around the Itasca State Park for the Saturday stages.

Practice was virtually washed out when a major thunderstorm passed through so it was a relief when the actual event took place in good, though cold, weather.

The first day was more like a Stig Blomqvist benefit when he and co-driver Ana Goni took six out of the seven stages. Despite such a dominating start he ended the day just nine seconds ahead of Pat Richard / Nathalie Richard, who took fastest time on one stage and came in second on a further four. Also showing well were Matt Iorio / Ole Holter lying third with

Pat Richard / Nathalie Richard lead until just a couple of miles of the finish.

Sans Thompson / Craig Marr win the Production Class.

Mark McElduff / Damien Irwin on the night stage.

Travis Pastrana / Christian Edstrom in fourth place. Ken Block / Alex Gelsomino had been well in the fight until having to retire after stage 4.

Day two started with a Parc Exposé and spectator super special stage in the Bemidji Speedway. Blomqvist started out continuing his winning times—being the only competitor to post a sub-minute time. But when they moved out to the forests it was Richard's time to dictate the pace. The afternoon session would consist of four forest stages including the twenty-mile Chad's Yump. Richard set fastest time on the next three stages; each time being shadowed by Blomqvist. Then on the final afternoon stage it was Blomqvist ahead of Richard.

Behind them Iorio and Pastrana were in their own private battle for third place—changing back and forward as the day went on.

As the teams came into service to prepare for the last four stages of the event, Richard had got ahead of Blomqvist, leading by fifteen seconds. Over two minutes back, Iorio was in third place and Pastrana fourth.

Richard took the first evening stage, Blomqvist the next, then Richard again. The differences between them were four seconds, two seconds and three seconds. While the fight was tight, Richard was holding his lead until the last stage—indeed until the last mile of the last stage—when his gearbox gave way forcing him to retire.

So, after a nail-biting finish, Stig Blomqvist / Ana Goni took the win. Behind them, Matt Iorio / Ole Holter were promoted to second and Travis Pastrana / Christian Edstrom came third.

With his win, Blomqvist extended his championship lead over Richard from just two points to twenty-three—the equivalent of more than one event.

Mark Utecht / Rob Bohn come in fifth overall.

Michael Wray / Donald DeRose in their Subaru Legacy.

Travis Pastrana, Christian Edstrom, Nathalie Richard and Pat Richard.

Matt Iorio / Ole Holter wow the spectators.

Doug Havir relaxes with a soda after retiring.

Tim Patterson / John Allen take Chad's jump.

Travis Hanson / Terry Hanson in their Toyota Celica.

Robert Olson / Conrad Ketelson took sixth in the open class.

Stig Blomqvist / Ana Goni one mile from the finish.

Brian Dondlinger / Dave Pards fight for grip.

Relaxing at Parc Exposé.

Ojibwe Forests Rally Schedule

Stage #	First Car	Stage Name	Miles
Friday, August 26			
	Rally Start		
1	18:08	Halverson Lake	5.48
	Service - Hubbard		
2	18:45	Spur 2	12.98
3	19:34	Parkway	4.95
4	19:57	Steamboat	3.84
	Service - Akeley		
5	21:46	Akeley Cutoff	9.48
6	22:16	Refuge	13.19
7	22:52	Blue Trail	11.08
Saturday, August 27			
8	14:04	Bemidji Speedway	0.64
	Service - Lake Itasca		
9	15:24	Heart Lake	3.81
10	15:49	Chad's Yump	20.11
11	16:47	Moulton Lake	6.92
12	17:20	Indian Creek	9.54
	Service - Osage		
13	19:28	Sockeye Lake	7.28
14	19:53	Anchor Cut	10.06
15	20:28	Sugar Bush	6.74
16	21:01	Perkins	12.29
	Rally Finish		

Doug Shepherd / Pete Gladysz take the crest into the Super Special.

Stig Blomqvist and Dave Whittock check out the Super Special Stage.

Ojibwe Forests Rally Results

O'all	Class	Class	Car #	Driver / Co-Driver	Car	SS-1	SS-2	SS-3	SS-4	SS-5	SS-6	SS-7	SS-8	SS-9	SS-10	SS-11	SS-12	SS-13	SS-14	SS-15	SS-16	Road Pnlty	Total
1	1	GN	65	Stig Blomqvist / Ana Goni	2003 Subaru Impreza WRX STi	5:20	12.47	4.42	3:34	10:06	13:08	12:21	0:00	4:16	20:46	6:12	8:49	6:01	8:15	7:36	13:56		18:49
2	1	O	18	Matt Iorio / Ole Holter	2001 Subaru Impreza	5:28	12:53	4:53	3:37	10:46	13:16	12:28	1:05	4:17	21:08	6:18	9:03	6:01	8:15	7:45	14:09		21:22
3	2	GN	199	Travis Pastrana / Christian Edstrom	2004 Subaru Impreza WRX STi	5:49	13:43	4:54	3:45	10:22	13:10	12:25	1:02	4:23	21:07	6:21	9:03	6:07	8:24	7:45	14:11		22:31
4	2	O	27	Chris Gilligan / Joe Peterson	1997 Mitsubishi EVO IV	5:41	13:35	4:57	3:46	11:13	13:56	12:53	1:04	4:31	21:59	6:37	9:28	6:20	8:46	8:04	14:30		27:20
5	3	GN	83	Mark Utecht / Rob Bohn	2002 Subaru WRX	5:39	13:35	4:57	3:48	11:16	13:51	12:55	1:04	4:33	21:57	6:39	9:31	6:22	8:39	8:04	15:14		28:05
6	4	GN	676	Mark McElduff / Damien Irwin	2002 Subaru WRX STi	5:40	13:50	5:04	3:52	11:05	14:13	13:48	1:02	4:39	21:49	6:38	9:26	6:19	8:54	8:23	15:36		30:17
7	3	O	52	Doug Shepherd / Pete Gladysz	2000	5:48	13:50	5:13	3:54	11:25	14:13	13:15	1:10	4:31	22:23	6:29	9:27	6:35	9:10	8:19	14:45		30:28
8	1	PGT	46	Matthew Johnson / Wendy Nakamoto	2003 Subaru WRX	5:50	13:53	5:02	3:53	11:30	14:27	13:09	1:03	4:36	22:59	6:46	9:36	6:23	8:59	8:27	15:24		31:57
9	2	PGT	153	Eric Langbien / Jeremy Wimpey	2002 Subaru WRX	5:57	14:21	5:17	4:01	11:40	15:02	13:38	1:04	4:36	22:43	6:42	9:44	6:36	9:04	8:21	15:12		33:58
10	4	O	93	Robert Olson / Conrad Ketelson	1999 Subaru 2.5 RS	5:57	14:32	5:20	4:08	11:56	15:10	14:01	1:15	4:34	22:53	6:44	9:50	6:47	9:26	8:31	15:32		36:37
11	5	GN	600	Finton McCarthy / Noel Gallagher	2002 Subaru WRX STi	6:01	14:29	5:16	4:01	11:30	14:30	13:40	1:08	4:45	23:21	7:20	10:16	7:09	10:16	8:56	16:27		39:06
12	3	PGT	595	John Cirisan / Josh Hamacher	2004 Subaru WRX	6:22	15:40	5:35	4:17	12:44	15:49	14:25	1:09	4:55	24:14	7:15	10:29	7:03	9:49	8:57	16:10		44:54
13	4	PGT	21	Yurek Cienkosz / Lukasz Szela	2002 Subaru Impreza	6:44	16:40	6:09	4:34	12:54	16:58	15:06	1:14	5:10	26:12	7:41	11:15	7:52	10:56	9:04	16:40		55:08
14	1	G5	60	Bruce Davis / Jimmy Brandt	2003 Dodge SRT-4	6:42	16:28	6:00	4:33	13:40	17:08	15:22	1:11	5:01	25:35	7:36	10:56	7:34	10:56	9:21	17:30		55:32
15	1	P	49	Sans Thompson / Craig Marr	2001 Dodge Neon	6:44	16:48	6:02	4:36	13:06	16:44	15:13	1:16	5:12	25:54	7:35	11:10	7:40	11:21	9:33	18:07		57:01
16	2	P	543	Mike Merbach / Jeff Feldt	1990 Volkswagon Jetta	6:51	17:00	6:22	4:38	13:42	17:05	15:38	1:12	5:20	27:46	8:00	11:22	8:00	11:23	10:16	17:38		2:14
		GN	1	Pat Richard / Nathalie Richard	2004 Subaru Impreza WRX STi	5:24	12:59	4:44	3:35	10:13	13:06	12:08	1:01	4:14	20:22	6:08	8:53	5:57	8:17	7:33			DNF
		PGT	507	Micah Wiitala / Jason Takkunen	1994 Mtsubishi Eclipse GSX	6:01	14:55	5:19	4:08	12:06	15:19	13:54	1:09	4:40	23:16	6:58							DNF
		O	88	Doug Havir / Scott Putnam	2004 Subaru WRX STi	5:47	13:53	5:04	3:55	11:48	15:13	13:45											DNF
		G2	122	Dennis Martin / Kim DeMotte	2000 Saturn	6:42	16:29	6:08	4:40	13:26	17:07	15:28											DNF
		O	107	Tim Paterson / John Allen	2005 Mitsubishi EVO VIII	5:56	13:52	5:05	4:00	11:23													DNF
		GN	43	Ken Block / Alex Gelsomino	2004 Subaru Impreza WRX STi	5:24	13:09	4:58	3:42														DNF
		O	207	Dave Hintz / Rick Hintz	2002 Subaru WRX	5:52																	DNF
		O	558	Jim Cox / Richard Donovan	2004 Chevrolet S10	6:14																	DNF

*Cars in Parc Exposé are led by the
David Sutton-prepared Subaru.*

Stig Blomqvist / Ana Goni drift uphill on Middle Cog.

COLORADO COG RALLY

Steamboat Springs, Colorado

September 17–18, 2005

The competition moved to the Rockies for penultimate round of the Rally America championship. Headquartered in Steamboat Springs, Colorado, the action took place some twenty miles to the west around Hayden.

The weather had been fine, causing the mud-based roads to dry rock hard. The combination of fast roads, dry surfaces and loose stones made this a high-risk event for drivers. Many were to crash out.

Pat Richard / Nathalie Richard had to win to keep alive their fight for the championship.

The morning of the first day was, as predicted, a duel between Richard and Stig Blomqvist / Ana Goni. On the first stage, Wolf Mountain, it was Blomqvist who took the honors over Travis Pastrana / Christian Edstrom. Richard came in third.

Richard came back with a two-second victory over Blomqvist on the eleven-mile Elkhead Loop. Then it was Blomqvist over Richard on Breeze Basin. The morning ended with the first Super Special run in the Hayden Fairgrounds. Here both

Pat Richard / Nathalie Richard win the event to keep their championship hopes alive.

Brooks Freehill / Brian McGuire put up a dust trail.

Mitch Williams / Alix Hakala cross the bridge on stage 2.

Wendy Nakamoto and Matt Johnson are interviewed for TV.

Blomqvist and Richard were bested by George Plsek / Jeff Burmeister and Antoine L'Estage / Marc Goldfarb.

So, by lunchtime, Blomqvist was leading Richard by six seconds with Pastrana in third. Consistent driving had put Lauchlin O'Sullivan / John Dillon in fourth.

The afternoon consisted of thirty-five miles of competition run over five stages including the scenic Middle Cog. The fight ran between the three leaders. On Middle Cog, Blomqvist and Richard shared best time. On the following stages, they each took the top spot twice. But by the end of the day, Richard had cut Blomqvist's lead to two seconds.

Pastrana was lying just fourteen seconds behind Richard, but on the first stage of the second day, he would take a slight right-hander too fast and roll out of the event, promoting Ken Block / Alex Gelsomino to third place. The day continued with Blomqvist and Richard exchanging fastest times until the second running of the Fairground stage. Both had problems with the tight turns of the superspecial allowing Matthew Johnson / Wendy Nakamoto to take fastest time from O'Sullivan / John Dillon.

As the teams went into the last three stages, Blomqvist was leading by 7.8 seconds but then Richard took the next two stages, clawing back to just 1.1 seconds behind Blomqvist.

As they started the last stage—Middle Cog 4—it was all to play for and, on this occasion, Richard was able to come through and take the stage by 1.5 seconds. Thus, after ninety-seven min-

Ana Goni and Stig Blomqvist chat with Dave Whittock (left).

Lauchlin O'Sullivan / John Dillon took third place.

Tanner Foust / Scott Crouch win the PGT Class.

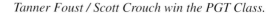

Lance Smith and Travis Pastrana share
a joke at the finish.

Nathalie Richard and Pat Richard celebrate.

*Nathan Conley /
Donny Conley on
stage 9.*

Colorado Cog Rally Schedule

Stage #	First Car	Stage Name	Miles
Saturday, September 17			
	8:01	Rally Start	
1	8:46	Wolf Mountain	4.07
2	9:48	Elkhead Loop	10.94
3	10:43	Breeze Basin	12.73
4	11:08	Super Special 1	0.92
		Service—Fairgrounds	
5	13:04	Middle Cog 1	6.78
6	13:25	Elkhead Flats 1	6.20
7	14:09	Stokes Gulch	12.71
		Service—Fairgrounds	
8	15:59	Middle Cog 2	5.21
9	17:01	Flow Mountain	4.06
Sunday, September 18			
10	9:46	Sage Creek 1	5.82
11	10:30	Middle Cog 3	6.78
12	10:51	Elkhead Flats 2	6.22
13	11:29	Super Special 2	0.92
		Service—Fairgrounds	
14	13:37	Sage Creek 2	5.85
15	14:15	Elkhead Flats 3	6.22
16	14:36	Middle Cog 4	5.21
	15:48	Rally Finish	

Ben Hanka is interviewed but wishes he was still in the event!

Antoine L'Estage / Marc Goldfarb have already seen the ditches.

Colorado Cog Rally Results

O'all	Class	Class	Car #	Driver / Co-Driver	Car	SS-1	SS-2	SS-3	SS-4	SS-5	SS-6	SS-7	SS-8	SS-9	SS-10	SS-11	SS-12	SS-13	SS-14	SS-15	SS-16	Road Penalties	Total
1	1	GN	1	Patrick Richard / Nathalie Richard	2004 Subaru Impreza	03:40.9	11:28.6	09:25.6	01:21.5	07:21.9	07:33.1	09:15.7	05:22.7	03:30.4	05:10.8	07:15.6	07:24.1	01:29.2	05:03.9	07:16.8	05:13.0		1:37:53.8
2	2	GN	65	Stig Blomqvist / Ana Goni	2003 Subaru Impreza STi	03:35.6	11:30.5	09:22.4	01:21.5	07:21.9	07:40.5	09:14.2	05:20.5	03:30.9	05:05.7	07:13.3	07:25.6	01:29.7	05:08.7	07:18.7	05:14.5		1:37:54.2
3	3	GN	90	Lauchlin O'Sullivan / John Dillon	2002 Mitsubishi EVO 7	03:44.2	11:50.6	09:42.1	01:25.2	07:34.3	07:47.8	09:58.1	05:34.3	03:41.3	05:17.6	07:21.5	07:33.6	01:27.9	05:19.5	07:34.2	05:26.1		1:41:18.3
4	4	GN	43	Ken Block / Alex Gelsomino	2004 Subaru Impreza WRX STi	03:46.6	11:49.9	09:45.0	01:26.6	07:35.2	07:40.1	09:40.3	05:32.2	03:39.1	05:24.8	07:27.6	07:36.9	01:33.3	05:17.9	07:35.9	05:24.1		1:41:24.5
5	1	PGT	429	Tanner Foust / Scott Crouch	2002 Subaru WRX	03:53.5	12:01.1	09:43.4	01:23.8	07:50.0	07:56.8	09:28.8	05:38.4	03:36.4	05:21.7	07:33.3	07:44.7	01:31.5	05:14.5	07:35.7	05:25.3		1:41:58.9
6	2	PGT	46	Matthew Johnson / Wendy Nakamoto	2003 Subaru WRX	03:50.1	12:12.1	09:31.8	01:25.5	07:36.1	07:51.3	09:48.9	05:41.7	03:41.7	05:22.2	07:30.9	07:39.7	01:26.0	05:20.2	07:36.4	05:29.6		1:42:04.2
7	1	O	30	George Plsek / Jeff Burmeister	2000 Mitsubishi Lancer EVO	03:50.4	12:01.9	09:57.9	01:20.3	07:43.6	07:53.2	09:47.2	05:35.6	03:45.8	05:32.5	07:30.8	07:33.7	01:30.8	05:26.2	07:38.3	05:29.7		1:42:37.9
8	3	PGT	153	Eric Langbein / Jeremy Wimpey	2002 Subaru WRX	03:59.8	12:09.7	09:53.8	01:27.5	07:51.5	08:03.5	09:50.4	05:41.3	03:48.7	05:25.1	07:36.3	07:50.9	01:30.1	05:33.2	07:48.0	05:38.4		1:44:08.2
9	5	GN	103	Wyeth Gubelmann / Cindy Krolikowski	2004 Subaru Impreza WRX	04:06.2	12:42.4	10:28.4	01:28.2	07:47.3	07:55.2	10:18.3	05:43.8	03:56.5	05:45.6	07:42.4	07:47.2	01:28.3	05:47.1	07:59.4	05:58.2		1:46:54.5
10	1	G5	407	Brooks Freehill / Brian McGuire	1992 Eagle Talon	04:20.8	13:48.8	11:49.3	01:34.7	08:52.4	08:50.3	11:24.3	06:35.2	04:31.6	05:59.6	08:17.1	08:29.1	01:38.9	06:08.1	08:44.7	06:16.8		1:57:21.7
11	2	O	24	Todd Moberly / Ray Moberly	2002 Subaru WRX	03:46.1	12:09.8	09:43.2	01:23.8	07:42.6	08:02.3	09:31.7	05:27.0	03:34.0	05:18.1	07:19.5	07:39.2	01:29.1	05:18.8	07:50.5			1:36:15.7
		GN	199	Travis Pastrana / Christian Edstrom	2004 Subaru Impreza WRX STi	03:37.2	11:36.6	09:26.7	01:22.2	07:25.3	07:34.6	09:17.8	05:22.1	03:32.0									DNF
		O	19	Antoine L'Estage / Marc Goldfarb	1999 Subaru WRX STi	03:41.2	15:22.1	09:32.5	01:20.5	07:39.4	07:56.0	09:29.8											DNF
		G2	418	Jimmy Keeney / Brian Moody	1996 Honda Civic	04:18.6	13:51.0	11:49.3	01:32.7	09:14.3	09:12.3	11:47.6											DNF
		O	39	Carl Jardevall / Janice Damitio	1997 Mitsubishi EVO 4	03:58.0	12:05.5	09:42.6	01:23.3	07:39.1	07:51.0												DNF
		GN	774	Otis Dimiters / Dominik Jozwiak	2002 Subaru WRX	03:51.2	12:20.0	09:43.6	01:24.0	07:37.6	08:42.5												DNF
		GN	600	Finton McCarthy / Noel Gallagher	2002 Subaru WRX STi	04:08.9	12:45.1	10:39.0	01:28.4	08:25.6	09:05.9												DNF
		O	107	Tim Paterson / Wayne Hartzler	2005 Mitsubishi Evo VIII	03:51.2	12:01.8	10:30.7	01:31.0														DNF

Left: Ken Block / Alex Gelsomino take fourth overall.

Wyeth Gubelmann / Cindy Krolikowski on the spectator stage.

Tom Lawless / Jason Gillespie win the event.

INTERNATIONAL RALLY NEW YORK

Monticello, New York

September 30–October 1, 2005

The Catskill area, 100 miles northwest of New York City, was the setting for the International Rally New York. The event was centered in Monticello—home of the Woodstock Festival. Day one would include four runnings of the Mighty M Gaming Super Special stage plus a visit to the gravel forest roads towards Narrowsburg twenty miles west of the city. For day two, the competition would return to Narrowsburg in the morning then move to Liberty in the north to take on asphalt county roads.

The strong entry included east coast regulars Tom Lawless / Jason Gillespie and Seamus Burke / Brian Sharkey. Peter Workum / Chrissie Beavis and Matt Iorio / Ole Holter had also entered.

The first two stages at the Mighty M Gaming Super Special put Lawless in the lead but as the teams went into the forests, it was Otis Dimiters / Alan Ockwell who took the first forest stage, Crystal Lake, four seconds ahead of Lawless then Iorio.

Right: Scott Wilburn / Carrie Wilburn take to the forests.

Teams gather at the Parc Exposé at Monticello Raceway.

Otis Dimiters / Alan Ockwell work to make up for lost time.

Below, left: It's an engine . . .

Seamus Burke / Brian Sharkey came in second in their newly built Mitsubishi.

Martin Donnelly / Sean Coffey would retire after stage 4.

Eugeniusz Michniuk / Cesare Fidler.

Victors celebrate! From left: Brian Sharkey, Seamus Burke, Tom Lawless, Jason Gillespie, Chrissie Beavis and Peter Workum.

Tom Lawless / Jason Gillespie in a full-power drift round the raceway.

Local residents enjoy the early morning show.

Noel Nash / Eddie Fries in the morning stages.

Martin O'Flynn / Bernard Obry win the SS2 Class.

International Rally New York Schedule

Stage #	FirstCar	Stage Name	Miles	Stage #	FirstCar	Stage Name	Miles
Friday, September 30				**Saturday, October 1**			
Rally Start				11	8:14	Cochecton Turnpike 1	5.72
1	13;03	Mighty M Gaming Super Special	0.50	12	8:33	Mortimer Schiff 2	6.57
2	13:48	Mighty M Gaming Super Special	0.46			Service - Narrowsburg	
3	14:16	Crystal Lake 1	6.55	13	9:36	Cochecton Turnpike 2	5.72
4	14:32	Davis Lake West 1	3.40	14	9:57	Camp Keowa	2.41
		Service - Narrowsburg				Service - Narrowsburg	
5	15:32	Crystal Lake 2	6.55	15	11:42	Mathias Weiden East 1	4.45
6	15:48	Davis Lake West 2	3.40	16	11:57	Blind Pond 1	3.03
		Service - Narrowsburg				Service - Narrowsburg	
7	17:19	Davis Lake East	3.60	17	12:54	Mathias Weiden East 2	4.45
8	17:32	Mortimer Schiff 1	6.57	18	13:09	Blind Pond 2	3.03
9	18:24	Mighty M Gaming Super Special	0.50			Service - Narrowsburg	
10	19:44	Mighty M Gaming Super Special	0.46	19	14:28	Mathias Weiden West	4.20
				20	15:22	Elk Pond 1	6.15
						Service - Liberty	
				21	16:27	Lenape Lake 1	5.84
				22	16:57	Elk Pond 2	6.15
						Service - Liberty	
				23	18:02	Lenape Lake 2	5.84
				24	18:32	Elk Pond 3	6.15
				25	19:43	Mighty M Gaming Super Special	0.50
						Rally Finish	

International Rally New York Results

STAGE TIMES (Minutes:Seconds)

O'all	Class	Class	Car #	Driver	Co-Driver	SS-1	SS-2	SS-3	SS-4	SS-5	SS-6	SS-7	SS-8	SS-9	SS-10	SS-11	SS-12	SS-13	SS-14	SS-15	SS-16	SS-17	SS-18	SS-19	SS-20	SS-21	SS-25	Road Points	Total
1	1	O4	2	Tom Lawless	Jason Gillespie	0:37	0:32	6:05	4:06	6:00	4:12	4:24	6:10	0:36	0:32	5:30	5:59	5:17	2:03	3:34	2:23	3:32	2:21	3:15	5:11	4:50	0:32		77:41
2	2	O4	1	Seamus Burke	Brian Sharkey	0:39	0:34	6:13	4:13	6:18	4:16	4:38	6:24	0:39	0:34	5:32	6:10	5:36	2:09	3:54	2:31	3:41	2:30	3:26	5:14	4:46	0:34		80:31
3	3	O4	3	Peter Workum	Chrissie Beavis	0:38	0:34	6:17	4:18	6:24	4:19	4:39	6:32	0:39	0:33	5:37	6:18	5:36	2:10	3:42	2:23	3:45	2:23	3:31	5:10	4:56	0:33		80:57
4	4	O4	12	Daniel O'Brien	Stephen Duffy	0:42	0:33	6:29	4:28	6:33	4:32	4:34	6:28	0:40	0:34	5:43	6:23	5:34	2:12	3:44	2:27	3:42	2:27	3:36	5:26	4:59	0:34	0:10	82:30
5	1	P1	20	Jeremy Drislane	Barry Goodman	0:43	0:35	6:33	4:21	6:38	4:27	4:41	6:25	0:38	0:34	5:35	6:03	5:35	2:11	4:10	2:23	4:06	2:45	3:47	5:41	5:13	0:35		83:39
6	1	SS2	25	Martin O'Flynn	Bernhard Obry	0:43	0:36	6:50	4:43	6:58	4:40	4:58	6:50	0:41	0:37	6:02	6:33	6:03	2:17	3:58	2:34	3:59	2:35	3:53	5:59	5:27	0:35	0:15	87:46
7	1	SS	18	Emilio Arce	Craig Thrall	0:43	0:36	6:34	4:50	6:50	4:51	4:58	6:56	0:42	0:37	6:03	6:42	5:52	2:21	4:13	2:43	4:07	2:44	3:52	5:48	5:20	0:39		88:01
8	1	SS1	17	Patrick Brennan	Donah O'Leary	0:40	0:35	6:30	4:32	9:15	4:37	5:14	6:40	0:38	0:34	6:00	6:40	5:43	2:16	4:01	2:31	4:12	2:41	3:35	5:22	4:53	0:33	0:25	88:07
9	1	P2	32	Dave Getchell	Erik Lee	0:43	0:38	6:58	4:42	6:57	4:53	4:55	7:11	0:45	0:40	6:13	6:59	6:10	2:24	4:16	2:48	4:10	2:45	3:57	5:59	5:22	0:38		90:03
10	2	P1	40	Fintan Seeley	Paddy McCague	1:00	0:35	7:03	4:52	7:15	4:58	4:56	7:19	0:43	0:36	6:07	6:55	5:49	2:26	4:00	2:34	3:56	2:30	3:43	5:34	5:15	0:37	2:25	91:08
11	3	P1	19	Donald Kennedy	Keith Kennedy	0:41	0:36	7:30	4:51	7:30	4:46	5:01	7:13	0:42	0:36	6:09	7:11	5:57	2:28	4:02	2:40	3:57	2:40	3:50	5:42	5:37	0:36	1:10	91:25
12	5	M2	27	Joshua Wimpey	Jeremy Wimpey	0:43	0:37	7:29	5:00	7:19	4:47	5:06	7:17	0:41	0:37	6:18	7:06	6:08	2:27	4:20	2:46	4:03	2:45	3:52	5:42	5:46	0:38		91:27
13	6	M2	31	Mark Lawrence	Robert Maciejski	0:43	0:38	7:03	4:52	7:13	4:54	5:16	7:35	0:44	0:39	6:35	6:58	6:06	2:25	4:17	2:53	4:11	2:48	3:54	5:44	5:41	0:38		91:47
14	2	SS2	38	Wojciech Okula	Adam Pelc	0:43	0:37	6:58	4:53	7:10	5:03	5:20	7:35	0:45	0:39	6:40	7:22	6:24	2:29	4:15	2:45	4:12	2:44	4:06	6:13	6:02	0:37		93:32
15	3	SS2	46	James McKiernan	Martin Shekleton	0:41	0:36	7:36	5:10	7:54	5:40	5:41	8:20	0:41	0:35	6:54	7:46	6:35	2:40	4:26	2:57	4:23	2:56	4:05	6:03	6:01	0:36		98:16
16	1	M1	47	Mike Hall	Dave Stockdill	0:47	0:39	7:51	5:13	7:45	5:12	5:44	7:48	0:45	0:39	6:36	7:44	6:35	2:34	4:31	2:56	4:23	2:55	4:12	6:23	6:22	0:40	0:05	98:19
17	2	SS	43	Joan Hoskinson	Jeff Secor	0:44	0:39	7:57	5:05	7:52	5:06	5:25	7:49	0:45	0:39	6:52	7:48	6:34	2:39	4:43	3:04	4:31	2:56	4:15	6:15	6:13	0:38		98:29
18	4	SS2	41	Eugeniusz Michniuk	Cesare Fiedler	0:42	0:34	7:36	4:53	7:45	5:07	5:13	7:48	0:38	0:35	6:38	7:27	6:25	2:29	4:16	2:50	4:03	2:41	3:55	6:01	6:10	0:34	4:40	99:00
19	5	SS2	33	Scott Wilburn	Carrie Wilburn	0:45	0:38	7:53	5:07	7:51	5:05	5:36	8:00	0:44	0:38	6:50	7:38	6:43	2:43	4:37	3:01	4:38	2:58	4:13	6:32	6:13	0:38		99:01
20	5	O4	15	Maciej Przybysz	Dominik Jozwiak	0:42	0:35	6:33	4:24	20:23	4:42	4:51	6:49	0:41	0:35	5:44	6:49	5:57	2:19	3:56	2:33	3:51	2:26	3:36	5:40	5:14	0:35	0:10	99:05
21	1	S.	37	Eric Heitkamp	Nick Lehner	0:43	0:37	8:00	4:56	7:58	5:10	5:09	7:52	0:42	0:37	6:36	7:45	6:17	2:34	4:15	2:47	4:11	2:44	3:52	6:01	5:50	0:36	5:20	100:32
22	2	M1	26	Greg Healey	John MacLeod	0:45	0:37	8:43	5:14	8:12	5:10	5:26	8:10	0:44	0:38	8:05	8:09	6:29	2:45	4:26	3:02	4:22	2:58	4:02	6:15	6:31	0:38	1:10	101:04
23	4	P1	39	Dan Brosnan	Chris King	0:44	0:37	8:08	5:13	8:16	5:16	5:30	7:52	0:42	0:38	6:57	7:45	6:51	2:38	4:23	2:46	4:21	2:47	4:05	6:04	6:09	0:35	5:00	103:17
24	3	M1	53	Luke Sorensen	John Iden	0:46	0:39	8:12	5:31	8:24	5:36	5:46	8:13	0:42	0:40	7:20	8:02	6:57	2:42	4:33	3:03	4:39	3:02	4:23	6:30	6:20	0:40	1:05	103:45
25	6	SS2	45	John O'Reilly	Connor Sheffangton	0:46	0:39	8:50	5:28	8:12	5:30	5:48	8:41	0:43	0:38	7:19	8:20	7:03	2:51	4:39	3:07	4:43	3:13	4:26	7:01	6:55	0:39	0:30	106:01
26	4	M1	36	Jon Hamilton	Ken Sabo	0:43	0:38	8:14	5:17	8:32	5:34	5:44	8:10	0:44	0:39	6:28	7:36	6:26	3:07	4:10	2:44	4:05	2:45	3:53	6:00	6:06	0:37	11:00	109:12
27	1	O2	29	Craig Hollingsworth	Jason Grahn	0:44	0:38	7:10	4:51	7:26	5:04	5:12	7:26	0:42	0:39	6:13	7:13	6:17	2:48	19:30	3:01	4:15	2:52	4:22	7:35	6:40	1:56	2:20	114:54
.		SS2	24	Martin Egan	Tommy Byrne	0:43	0:35	7:03	4:45	7:18	4:57	5:09	7:20	0:43	0:38	6:32	17:53	6:55	6:06	4:16	2:40	4:45	2:51	3:56	5:46	6:36		0:15	DNF
.		O4	9	Patrick Lilly	Bernard Farrell	0:38	0:33	6:55	4:35	6:56	4:36	4:33	6:46	0:38	0:33	5:48	6:43	5:55	2:24	4:10	2:38	4:06	2:38	3:35	5:38			0:05	DNF
.		P1	16	Gerard Coffey	Dave Dooley	0:39	0:32	6:35	4:34	6:51	4:34	4:42	6:36	0:37	0:33	5:39	6:28					3:57	2:32	3:32	5:25	5:01	0:35	0:20	DNF
.		O4	4	Matt Iorio	Ole Holter	0:41	0:34	6:12	4:12	6:08	4:11	4:22	6:15	0:40	0:34	5:17	6:07	5:22	2:05	4:05	2:36	3:41	2:32						DNF
.		M2	28	Colin Bombara	Kristie Bombara	0:41	0:36	7:03	4:42	11:04						6:20	7:27	6:03	2:34	4:08	2:56	4:05	2:43	3:46	5:36	5:28	0:36	0:05	DNF
.		M2	51	Ty Crowley	Mike Spillane	0:48	0:41	8:19	5:56							7:42	9:15	7:14	3:00	4:47	3:05	4:43	3:03	4:26	6:40	6:24	0:40	3:00	DNF
.		GN	14	Otis Dimiters	Alan Ockwell	0:37	0:33	6:01	4:06	6:00	8:47	4:20	6:05	0:37	0:33	5:19	5:55	5:27	2:05	3:40	2:24								DNF
.		O4	10	Noel Nash	Eddie Fries	0:40	0:33	6:16	4:22	6:18	4:31	4:37	6:23	0:38	0:33	5:27	6:20	5:47	2:20	4:04	2:29								DNF
.		M2	52	David Furey	Brian Heneghan	0:43	0:38	8:08	5:17	7:54	5:05			0:46	0:38			6:56	2:42	5:05	3:26							2:05	DNF
.		GN	11	David Anton	Robbie Durant	0:40	0:33	6:15	4:20	6:18	4:27	4:30	6:15	0:40	0:34	15:36													DNF
.		O4	6	Patrick Farrell	Kierian McElhinney	0:38	0:34	6:15	4:36			4:38		0:39		5:31	6:15	5:27	2:06		2:34								DNF
.		SS2	42	Michael Cosgrove	Paul Treanor	0:42	0:37	7:40	4:58	7:43	5:01	5:38	8:14	0:43	0:37													0:10	DNF
.		P1	22	Scott Gardner	C Mantopoulos	0:53	0:34	6:27	4:27	6:46	4:37	4:58	8:44	0:45	0:35														DNF
.		O4	21	Blake Yoon	Robert Amato	0:41	0:36	6:43	4:32	6:42	4:31	4:44	6:44	0:41	0:37														DNF
.		M2	48	Larry Duane	Eamonn Sweeney	0:45	0:40	7:50	5:12	7:59	5:07	5:31																0:10	DNF
.		SS	44	Donal McGivney	Noel Gallagher	0:42	0:36	7:09	4:51	6:47																			DNF
.		P1	54	Martin Donnelly	Sean Coffey	0:39	0:33	6:33	4:26																			1:20	DNF
.		O4	23	Cyril Kearney	Samantha Smyth	0:40	0:34	17:12																				0:05	DNF
.		O2	35	Robin Jones	William Sekella																								DNF
.		O2	30	Bruce Davis	Jim Brandt																								DNF
.		P1	7	Adrian McElvanney	Paul Goodman																								DNF
.		GN	5	Ken Block	Alex Gelsomino																								DNF

Dave Getchell / Erik Lee get some height.

*Chris Gilligan / Joe Petersen
jump to second in Open Class.*

LAKE SUPERIOR PRO RALLY
Houghton, Michigan
October 21–22, 2005

The final round of the Rally America championship took place in the forests around Houghton in the Upper Peninsula of Michigan. There was still all to play for. The championship leaders, Stig Blomqvist / Ana Goni in their David Sutton-prepared Subaru had not entered. So the math was simple. If Pat Richard / Nathalie Richard won the event they would take the championship. Any other result would put them second.

An interesting entry came from Alfredo de Dominicis / Massimo Daddoveri, visiting from Italy and driving a Mitsubishi.

The organizers had been unable to get approval for the roads they traditionally run in the Ottawa National Forest and so, with just a few days to the event, had had to reschedule the first day—reducing the planned stages from seven to six and moving to the area south of L'Anse thirty miles south of Houghton.

The first challenge was Herman South—a smooth twisty road through Copper Country State Forest.

Fintan Seeley / Paddy McCague
in the fall colors.

Erik Payeur / Adam Payeur briefly lose the road.

Travis Pastrana concentrates on the road ahead.

Richard came out of the starting gate fast—taking a twenty-second lead from Ken Block / Alex Gelsomino and Matt Iorio / Ole Holter. Menge Creek, the second stage, showed that Richard was not going to take this event without a fight. Iorio won the stage first from Travis Pastrana / Christian Edstrom, then Richard.

After service, the second running of Herman South went to Pastrana from Richard then de Dominicis. That sequence was maintained for stage 4, but Richard came back to win the last two stages of the day—taking fastest time first from Pastrana then Iorio.

As the teams headed back to Houghton, Richard had established a thirty-three-second lead over Pastrana, followed by de Dominicis

The Saturday started cold and wet. The teams were to compete in eight stages consisting of forty-one competitive miles around the farthest tip of the Keweenaw peninsula. There would be three gravel stages before the teams tackled the asphalt Brockway with its fast jumps.

Russell Hodges / Mike Rossey flying . . .   *flying . . .*   *flying . . .*

Gratiot Lake, the first stage of the day and eighth in the schedule, showed that Richard could not depend on his thirty-three-second cushion. The stage was taken by Iorio then Block followed by Pastrana. Richard came in fourth ceding eight seconds to Iorio. On Delaware, the ninth stage, Richard came back with a win from de Dominicis then Block. Then Burma was taken by Block over Iorio and Richard. On the next two stages, de Dominicis, acclimatizing quickly to the American roads, took two wins over Richard.

So at service, after five stages of the second day, Richard had extended his lead over Pastrana to thirty-nine seconds. Pastrana had a thirty-three-second cushion from Block then Iorio.

With three stages left Richard was in a position to drive easier to conserve his car and ensure the event victory. He came in second on the next two stages and, finally, sixth on the last stage. The stage wins went to Iorio and de Dominicis.

As the teams headed back to Houghton for the formal finish, it was Pat Richard / Nathalie Richard who had won the event by thirty-five seconds over Travis Pastrana / Christian Edstrom. Third

. . . and finally, they make a single-wheel landing.

Ken Block / Alex Gelsomino jump into the night.

and fourth went to Matt Iorio / Ole Holter and Ken Block / Alex Gelsomino.

Through his win at LSPR, Pat Richard took the 2005 Rally America Drivers Championship by four points from Stig Blomqvist. For the co-drivers, Ana Goni, who had not competed with Blomqvist on one of the events, was twenty-four points behind the 2005 champion, Nathalie Richard.

Tanner Foust / Scott Crouch won the PGT Class.

Micah Witaza / Jason Takkunen hit the water.

John Cirisan / Josh Hamacher on the practice stage.

Otis Dimiters / Peter Monin would retire at the end of the first day.

Matt Johnson / Wendy Nakamoto.

Dave Lafavor / Chris Huntington in their Eagle Talon.

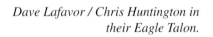

OOPS! Tim Stevens / Jeff Hagan.

Lake Superior Pro Rally Schedule

Stage #	First Car	Stage Name	Miles
Friday, October 21			
	16:01	Rally Start	
1	17:14	Herman South 1	7.23
2	18:06	Menge Creek North	7.12
		Service - L'Anse	
3	19:45	Herman South 2	7.23
4	20:40	Baraga Plains North	4.54
		Service - L'Anse	
5	22:12	Menge Creek South	7.10
6	23:02	Herman North	7.25
7	Cancelled		
Saturday, October 22			
8	11:37	Gratiot Lake 1	8.22
9	12:15	Delaware 1	4.28
		Service - Mt. Bohemia	
10	13:21	Burma 1	4.55
11	13:44	Brockway	3.18
12	14:21	Delaware 2	4.28
		Service - Mt. Bohemia	
13	15:52	Burma 2	4.55
		Service - Mt. Bohemia	
14	16:59	Delaware 3	4.27
15	17:32	Gratiot Lake 2	8.13
	18:44	Rally Finish	

Henry Krolikowski / Cindy Krolikowski place third in Open Class.

Jake Himes / Matti Himes spread water on stage 1.

Lake Superior Pro Rally Results

O'all	Class	Class	Car #	Driver / Co-Driver	Car	SS-1	SS-2	SS-3	SS-4	SS-5	SS-6	SS-8	SS-9	SS-10	SS-11	SS-12	SS-13	SS-14	SS-15	Road Penalties	Total
1	1	GN	1	Patrick Richard / Nathalie Richard	2002 Subaru Impreza WRX	06:52.0	06:33.1	07:22.1	03:41.9	06:42.3	07:12.0	07:43.2	03:27.5	05:03.1	02:36.4	03:30.7	04:58.1	03:32.2	08:34.5		1:17:49.1
2	2	GN	199	Travis Pastrana / Christian Edstrom	2004 Subaru Impreza WRX Sti	07:17.7	06:31.7	07:15.4	03:37.4	06:42.5	07:32.0	07:39.4	03:30.9	05:07.1	02:37.8	03:31.6	05:02.7	03:34.8	08:23.3		1:18:24.3
3	1	O	18	Matt Iorio / Ole Holter	1997 Subaru Impreza	07:11.8	06:26.1	08:12.1	03:45.7	06:43.0	07:25.4	07:35.1	03:31.7	05:02.0	02:37.5	03:31.9	04:50.1	03:35.0	08:02.6		1:18:30.0
4	3	GN	43	Ken Block / Alex Gelsomino	2004 Subaru Impreza WRX STi	07:11.8	06:33.5	07:28.1	03:45.4	06:56.2	07:46.0	07:35.4	03:29.0	04:59.1	02:40.3	03:31.3	05:01.1	03:35.4	08:30.4		1:19:03.0
5	4	GN	77	Alfredo De Dominicis / Massimo Daddoveri	1997 Mitsubishi Lancer Evo 7	07:20.7	06:43.2	07:25.2	03:43.6	06:45.5	07:32.0	07:53.1	03:28.5	05:08.0	02:36.2	03:27.7	05:06.1	03:29.1	08:32.3		1:19:11.2
6	1	PGT	429	Tanner Foust / Scott Crouch	2003 Subaru WRX	07:29.2	06:47.8	07:47.8	03:51.1	07:00.2	07:49.4	08:02.5	03:39.3	05:08.6	02:46.1	03:41.8	05:09.5	03:40.5	08:32.8		1:21:26.6
7	2	O	27	Chris Gilligan / Joe Petersen	1997 Mitsubishi Lancer Evo 7	07:22.0	06:45.4	07:33.4	03:46.9	07:00.2	07:37.8	08:04.1	03:29.1	05:21.1	02:39.5	03:33.6	05:32.0	03:46.9	09:14.1		1:21:46.1
8	2	PGT	46	Matt Johnson / Wendy Nakamoto	2003 Subaru WRX	07:24.2	06:47.2	07:45.2	03:50.8	07:16.5	07:48.5	07:52.8	03:35.0	05:17.0	02:41.7	03:41.4	05:19.7	03:38.8	09:15.4		1:22:14.2
9	1	G5	52	Doug Shepherd / Pete Gladysz	2004 Dodge SRT 4	07:22.5	06:44.8	07:47.0	04:16.2	07:04.0	08:05.0	08:26.7	03:38.7	05:27.0	02:41.0	03:42.5	06:11.0	03:37.5	08:36.3		1:23:40.2
10	3	O	44	Henry Krolikowski / Cindy Krolikowski	2000 Subaru WRX	07:30.0	06:55.5	07:51.9	04:00.5	07:29.1	08:05.0	08:33.0	03:44.4	05:30.0	02:45.1	03:46.0	05:38.0	03:51.1	09:04.8		1:24:45.2
11	5	GN	964	David Anton / Alan Ockwell	2002 Subaru WRX STi	07:33.7	07:11.3	08:00.8	04:22.9	07:27.8	08:16.2	08:26.5	03:52.6	05:46.0	02:44.1	03:54.0	05:41.0	03:53.7	09:07.2		1:26:17.8
12	6	GN	600	Fintan McCarthy / Noel Gallagher	2002 WRX STi	07:56.3	07:06.4	08:01.0	04:03.4	07:25.6	08:12.1	08:39.6	03:51.9	05:37.0	03:00.8	03:53.7	05:28.0	03:58.6	09:03.4		1:26:17.9
13	3	PGT	153	Eric Langbein / Jeremy Wimpey	2002 Subaru WRX	07:32.3	06:50.9	07:58.4	04:32.1	07:41.4	08:29.5	08:35.7	03:46.6	05:25.0	02:48.1	03:48.5	05:39.0	03:50.5	09:30.0		1:26:28.0
14	7	GN	565	Russell Hodges / Mike Rossey	1995 Subaru Impreza	07:53.6	07:13.5	08:11.0	04:11.9	07:42.2	08:22.6	08:52.1	03:55.8	05:42.0	02:43.0	03:59.0	05:47.0	04:03.6	09:39.5		1:28:16.8
15	4	O	521	Chris Czyzio / Bob Martin	1991 Mitsubishi Eclipse GSX	08:07.7	07:26.7	08:45.5	04:25.5	08:00.5	08:49.7	09:35.7	04:10.8	06:08.0	03:06.3	04:10.3	06:15.0	04:08.5	09:56.5		1:33:06.7
16	1	G2	507	Micah Witala / Jason Takkunen	1998 Saturn SL2	08:27.3	07:32.3	08:58.7	04:22.7	08:02.8	09:02.7	09:42.5	04:17.2	06:00.0	03:13.5	04:21.1	06:03.0	04:14.4	10:05.6		1:34:23.8
17	1	P	543	Mike Merbach / Jeff Feldt	1990 Volkswagen Jetta	08:30.0	08:01.3	08:48.5	04:29.4	08:21.0	09:06.3	09:26.3	04:18.0	05:57.0	03:07.5	04:28.2	06:03.0	04:22.2	09:59.0		1:34:55.7
18	2	G2	587	Matt Johnston / Alex Kihurani	1992 Honda Civic	08:37.0	08:18.5	09:09.1	04:42.0	08:25.1	08:48.1	09:38.8	04:23.8	06:12.0	03:13.3	04:22.7	06:15.0	04:23.9	10:29.0		1:36:58.3
19	5	O	558	Jim Cox / Ryan Lamothe	2004 Chevrolet S10	08:13.2	07:42.7	08:49.9	04:18.5	08:19.4	09:08.7	09:25.8	04:27.9	07:47.0	05:29.3	07:32.9	07:50.0	04:36.7	12:57.2		1:46:39.2
20	4	PGT	21	Yurek Cienkosz / Lukasz Szela	2002 Subaru Impreza RS	08:39.4	07:54.7	08:52.9	04:49.6	08:30.7	09:42.8	09:45.3	04:25.9	06:12.0	03:14.4	04:32.6	06:14.0	04:33.5	10:05.3	12:00.0	1:49:33.1
		PGT	595	John Cirisan / Josh Hamacher	2004 Subaru WRX	08:11.9	07:23.4	08:22.1	04:15.4	07:54.4	08:25.3	08:49.0	03:55.0	05:31.0	02:55.6	03:54.6					DNF
		P	49	Sans Thompson / Craig Marr	2000 Dodge Neon	08:27.0	07:55.1	08:47.6	04:25.0	08:16.7	08:42.0	09:39.4	04:26.6	05:58.0	03:08.2	04:51.0					DNF
		PGT	82	Joan Hoskinson / Jimmy Brandt	2000 Subaru Impreza RS	09:11.0	08:16.4	09:13.1	04:36.6	08:38.7	09:20.4	10:14.1	04:32.3								DNF
		O	868	Gerard Coffey / Dave Dooley	2006 Mitsubishi Evo 8	07:30.6	06:48.7	07:51.0	03:50.1	07:19.5	07:59.7										DNF
		GN	774	Otis Dimiters / Peter Monin	2002 Subaru WRX Sti	07:34.6	06:56.4	08:07.6	05:04.3	07:05.1	07:43.6										DNF
		G5	83	Mark Utecht / Rob Bohn	1988 Ford Mustang	07:42.6	07:12.0	08:20.8	04:10.9	13:39.4	09:15.7										DNF
		PGT	19	Tim Penasack / Marc Goldfarb	2002 Subaru Impreza WRX	07:36.0	07:04.6	08:02.3	04:01.3	08:09.2											DNF
		PGT	884	Tim Stevens / Jeff Hagan	2002 Subaru Impreza	08:11.8	07:27.6	08:46.9	04:21.5												DNF
		O	99	Fintan Seeley / Paddy McCague	2002 Subaru WRX	07:59.2	07:04.4														DNF
		O	93	Bob Olson / Ryan Johnson	1999 Subaru RS	07:39.0															DNF
		GN	676	Mark McElduff / Damien Irwin	2002 Subaru WRX STi																DNF

Pat Richard / Nathalie Richard lift a wheel.

Brad Morris / Ryan Gutile create a dust trail.

RAMADA EXPRESS
INTERNATIONAL RALLY
Laughlin, Nevada
December 9–11, 2005

The final round of the U.S. Rally Championship took place in the scenic and seductive surroundings of the Nevada casino city of Laughlin. For the eighth running of the event the organizers had attracted a wide entry.

Following wins in Chattanooga and Monticello, Tom Lawless was leading the championship by ten points and just needed a good result in Laughlin to secure the championship. His regular co-driver, Jason Gillespie held a similar lead in the co-driver standings. Determined to make sure their task would not be too easy, Seamus Burke / Eddie Fries had also travelled across country to compete. Going into the event, second place for the championship was jointly held by last year's winning team, Peter Workum / Chrissie Beavis, with Matt Iorio / Ole Holter. For this event, Iorio had switched allegiance from the usual Subaru to a Mitsubishi Evo. Another interest-

Tom Lawless / Jason Gillespie on
the Grand Canyon Stage.

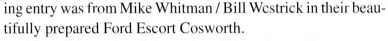

Marco Pasten / Jennifer Imai dig into the dust.

ing entry was from Mike Whitman / Bill Westrick in their beautifully prepared Ford Escort Cosworth.

The talking point of the weekend, though, was the two overseas entries. The 2004 New Zealand champions, Sam Murray / Anton Cheetham, had brought their Subaru while Flip Van Zutphen / Theo Badenberg had imported a Lancia HG Integrale from the Netherlands.

The first day of the event would use roads that were new to the event with some interesting "twists". Blake Ranch stage and the connected Cane Springs stage included a brief high-speed drive around the corral of the private ranch of the Fisher family. These stages were followed by a wonderful find called 17 Mile Road: which made a twelve-mile stage of twists and jumps through the Arizona desert.

On the second day, the event would use the well-known roads around the Grand Canyon: Grand Canyon, Black Canyon and Diamond Creek. Finally, on the Sunday, the teams would have a short drive to the edge of Laughlin for the traditional Spectator Super Special stage. The drivers would compete head-to-head for three runs around the stage.

Nathan Conley / Brandye Monks have a new rear wing.

From the start it was clear that this would be a competition between Lawless and Murray. Lawless took Blake Ranch by less than a second then Murray took the next two stages from Lawless. At the end of 17 Mile Road, the teams turned round and retraced the roads doing the three stages in reverse. The first two positions were also reversed with Lawless winning the first two and Murray taking Blake Ranch. By the end of the day, Lawless was leading Murray by less than 5 seconds. Two minutes behind them, there was an equally tight battle between Whitman and Burke. Workum had been in contention through the day but lost twelve minutes on Cane Springs 2 - putting him out of a podium position.

The second day saw the battle between Lawless and Murray being resolved in the Irishman's favour. Although

Sam Murray / Anton Cheetham
(2004 New Zealand Champions).

Murray was always in contention, it was Lawless who took five of the six stages. Iorio took fastest time on the first running of Diamond Creek.

After three runs at the Super Special stage, the overall winner was Tom Lawless / Jason Gillespie ahead of Sam Murray / Anton Cheetham. In third came Seamus Burke / Eddie Fries then Matt Iorio / Ole Holter.

Their overall win also confirmed Tom Lawless and Jason Gillespie as championship winners—having won every event they had entered.

Dennis Chizma / Andrew Cushman
drift on stage 6.

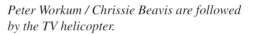

Peter Workum / Chrissie Beavis are followed by the TV helicopter.

Blake Yoon / John Dillon race a Porsche on the Super Special Stage.

A photographer in the evening light.

Craig Hollingsworth / Jason Grahn retired after stage 8.

Seamus Burke and Matt Iorio wait for their turns at the Super Special.

Tom Lawless / Jason Gillespie on the start ramp.

Tom Lawless won the event and the championship.

Mike Whitman / Bill Westrick gave their Ford Escort a successful outing.

Michael Taylon / J. Taylor in a Ford Ranger.

Ole Holter watches the action.

Ramada Express International Rally Schedule

Stage #	First Car	Stage Name	Miles		Stage #	First Car	Stage Name	Miles
Friday, December 9					**Saturday, December 10**			
	8:31	Rally Start				7:00	Day Start	
1	10:14	Blake Ranch East	3.5		9	9:33	Grand Canyon South	18.9
2	10:47	Cane Springs East	8.4		10	10:01	Black Canyon South	8.7
	11:27	Service - Wikieup				10:35	Service - Buck and Doe	
3	13:00	17 Mile Road West	12.4		11	11:43	Diamond Creek In	16.8
		(Stages 4 and 5 cancelled)			12	13:03	Diamond Creek Out	16.8
6	14:12	17 Mile Road East	12.4			13:41	Service - Buck and Doe	
	15:05	Service - Wikieup			13	14:54	Black Canyon North	8.8
7	16:38	Cane Springs West	8.4		14	15:27	Grand Canyon North	18.9
8	17:16	Blake Ranch West	3.5			18:27	Day Finish	
	18:56	Day Finish						
					Sunday, December 11			
						9:00	Day Start	
					15	10:00	Super Stage 1	1.8
					16	11:30	Super Stage 2	1.8
					17	13:00	Super Stage 3	1.8
						13:05	Rally Finish	

Seamus Burke / Eddie Fries
take third overall.

Ramada Express International Rally Results

Car #	Driver	Co-Driver	Car	SS-1	SS-2	SS-3	SS-6	SS-7	SS-8	SS-9	SS-10	SS-11	SS-12	SS-13	SS-14	SS-15	SS-16	SS-17	Road Points	Overall Total
3	Tom Lawless	Jason Gillespie	Mitsubishi Evo 8	3.08	6.41	9.44	9.59	6.82	3.06	14.75	7.50	12.94	13.08	7.60	15.24	1.58	1.58	3.25	0	115.92
7	Sam Murray	Anton Cheetham	Subaru Impreza	3.09	6.26	9.09	9.42	7.17	3.45	14.76	7.53	12.92	13.53	7.83	17.36	1.62	1.62	3.23	0	118.88
2	Seamus Burke	Eddie Fries	Mitsubishi Evo 8	3.61	7.47	9.51	9.68	7.21	3.35	15.24	8.38	12.93	13.20	7.89	18.62	1.72	1.61	3.27	0	123.69
4	Matt Iorio	Ole Holter	Mitsubishi Evo 7	3.11	6.48	9.60	10.95	9.01	3.96	15.40	7.71	12.89	13.71	8.00	18.43	1.68	1.60	5.25	0	127.78
8	Mike Whitman	Bill Westrick	Ford Escort Cosworth	3.19	6.60	9.73	10.22	7.66	3.41	15.48	8.67	14.34	15.09	7.96	20.23	1.68	1.65	3.36	0	129.27
14	Dennis Chizma	Andrew Cushman	Porsche 964	3.39	7.08	10.16	10.01	8.08	3.87	16.37	8.49	14.08	15.00	8.96	20.81	1.74	1.74	3.45	0	133.23
11	Blake Yoon	John Dillon	Mitsubishi Galant	3.53	6.92	11.99	10.84	9.23	4.00	16.65	8.22	14.59	14.45	8.77	21.99	1.76	1.71	3.51	1.4	139.56
1	Peter Workum	Chrissie Beavis	Subaru Impreza	3.16	6.63	9.95	10.67	18.68	4.05	15.93	8.07	13.20	14.38	8.41	20.17	1.68	1.61	3.34	0	139.93
23	Jimmy Keeney	Brian Moody	Honda Civic	3.52	7.61	10.81	10.98	8.23	4.32	17.46	9.10	16.17	15.88	9.74	23.75	1.92	1.88	3.71	0	145.08
21	Jeff Rados	Guido Hamacher	Ford Ranger	3.89	7.81	11.36	11.90	9.02	4.23	17.99	9.00	15.42	16.60	10.13	24.15	2.03	1.79	3.57	0	148.89
15	Doug Robinson	Sue Robinson	VW Golf	3.71	7.83	11.11	11.38	9.44	4.34	18.53	9.63	15.99	17.00	10.04	23.73	1.83	1.92	3.82	0	150.30
19	Mike Masano	Linda Masano	Toyota Corolla	3.90	8.38	11.51	11.78	9.54	4.41	18.34	9.08	15.73	17.27	10.34	22.81	1.93	1.87	3.81	0	150.70
43	Brad Morris	Ryan Gutile	Mitsubishi Lancer	3.63	7.69	11.74	11.75	9.38	4.54	18.30	9.89	15.68	17.06	10.46	23.50	1.96	1.98	3.97	0	151.53
25	Larry Gross	Doug Young	Toyota Corolla	3.88	8.22	11.49	11.62	9.58	4.43	18.94	9.62	16.19	17.34	10.62	22.20	1.99	1.99	3.98	0	152.09
10	Doug Chernis	Alan Perry	Subaru Impreza	3.56	7.67	10.85	11.14	8.34	3.85	17.16	15.90	17.12	17.64	10.53	26.41	1.76	1.79	3.53	0	157.25
9	Flip Van Zutphen	Theo Badenberg	Lancia HF Integrale	3.99	8.60	11.84	12.34	9.83	4.39	19.30	9.49	16.68	17.87	11.17	25.25	1.74	1.78	3.62	2.4	160.29
33	Nick Hudson	Brian Hudson	Toyota Corolla	3.94	8.16	12.02	12.13	9.73	4.74	19.41	12.97	17.32	18.90	11.04	23.64	1.96	2.02	4.07	0	162.05
34	Lisa Klassen	Kala Rounds	Toyota Corolla	3.80	8.12	11.71	11.59	9.71	4.29	19.26	9.77	16.77	18.87	26.99	37.95	2.38	4.00	3.99	0	189.20
37	Marco Pasten	Jennifer Imai	Toyota Corolla	3.92	7.87	11.74	11.97	9.61	7.39	19.05	9.80	18.08	20.23			1.95	2.03	4.17	6.2	DNF
28	Christopher Hill	Colver Sonnentag	Mazda 323 GTX	3.53	7.20	10.73	11.19	9.13	3.99	25.62	13.33	16.51	114.39			1.90	1.88	3.75	3.2	DNF
31	Cem Akdeniz	Mustafa Samli	Subaru Impreza	3.88	8.52	11.60	11.53	9.79	4.25	18.21	9.19	15.81	16.83	10.24		1.85	1.89	3.79	0	DNF
5	Leon Styles	Mark McAllister	Subaru Impreza	3.24	6.83	10.03	10.75	8.60	3.94										0	DNF
16	Craig Hollingsworth	Jason Grahn	VW Jetta GLI	3.63	7.43	10.81	10.95	8.70	3.84										0	DNF
22	Tony Chavez	Bret Robinson	VW Golf GTI	3.78	7.70	11.00	11.26	9.16	4.29										0	DNF
13	Erik Lyden	Jay Socha	Subaru Legacy	3.32	6.94	10.29													0	DNF
6	Stephan Verdier	Alan Ockwell	Subaru Impreza	3.13															0	DNF
39	Scott Clark	Marie Boyd	Subaru																0	DNF

Flip van Zutphen / Theo Badenberg visited from the Netherlands.

Rally America Championship

Overall Positions

#	Driver Name	Home Base	Points	#	Co-Driver Name	Home Base	Points
1	Patrick Richard	Garibaldi Highlands, B.C., Canada	121	1	Nathalie Richard	St-Jean-sur-Richelieu, Quebec, Canada	124
2	Stig Blomqvist	Northants, United Kingdom	117	2	Ana Goni	Northants, United Kingdom	100
3	Matthew Iorio	Millis, Massachusetts	79	3	Ole Holter	Long Beach, California	80
4	Ken Block	Encinitas, California	65	4	Christian Edstrom	New York, New York	73
5	Travis Pastrana	Annapolis, Maryland	61	5	Alessandro Gelsomino	Santa Clarita, California	62
6	Tanner Foust	Steamboat Springs, Colorado	39	6	Scott Crouch	Boulder, Colorado	44
7	Chris Gilligan	Cornelius, North Carolina	35	7	Wendy Nakamoto	Sacramento, California	40
8	Matthew Johnson	Apex, North Carolina	33	8	Joe Petersen	Rubicon, Wisconsin	35
9	Doug Shepherd	Plymouth, Michigan	25	9	Cynthia Krolikowski	Wyandotte, Michigan	34
10	Mark McElduff	Chicago, Illinois	24	10	Jeremy Wimpey	Herndon, Virginia	26
10	Otis Dimiters	Great Neck, New York	24	11	Rob Bohn	Noblesville, Indiana	25
12	Stephan Verdier	Huntington Beach, California	23	12	Jeffrey Becker	New York, New York	23
12	Eric Langbein	Potomac, Maryland	23	13	Peter Monin	Norwalk, Connecticut	20
14	Mark Utecht	Stacy, Minnesota	22	14	Jeffrey Burmeister	St Louis Park, Minnesota	19
15	Jonathan Bottoms	Buffalo, New York	21	14	Carolyn Bosley	Hinesburg, Vermont	19
16	Henry Krolikowski	Wyandotte, Michigan	18	16	John Dillon	Thousand Oaks, California	18
17	Wyeth Gubelmann	Placerville, Colorado	17	17	John Allen	Bainbridge Island, Washington	16
18	James Cox	Hamel, Minnesota	16	18	Craig Marr	Chico, California	15
19	Lauchlin O'Sullivan	San Francisco, California	14	18	Jason Gillespie	Maspeth, New York	15
19	Douglas Havir	Golden Valley, Minnesota	14	20	Peter Watt	Peterborough, Ontario, Canada	13
21	George Plsek, Jr.	Del Mar, California	13	20	Pete Gladysz	Troy, Michigan	13
21	Ramana Lagemann	Somerville, Massachusetts	13	20	Alexander Kihurani	Mohnton, Pennsylvania	13
21	Sans Thompson	Grass Valley, California	13	23	Jimmy Brandt	Lake Odessa, Michigan	9
21	William Bacon	Chelmsford, Massachusetts	13	23	Jeff Feldt	Kaukauna, Wisconsin	9
25	Matt Johnston	Rockford, Michigan	12	25	Noel Gallagher	Yonkers, New York	8
26	Martin Donnelly	Pearl River, New York	10	26	Pamela McGarvey	Columbus, Ohio	7
26	Tim Paterson	Redmond, Washington	10	26	Andrew Coombs	Mercerville, New Jersey	7

Rally America Championship

Overall Positions

Driver

#	Name	Home Base	Points
26	Robert Olson	Eden Prairie, Minnesota	10
29	Michael Merbach	Appleton, Wisconsin	9
30	Fintan McCarthy	Chicago, Illinois	8
30	Bruce Davis	Granite Bay, California	8
32	Joan Hoskinson	Thunder Bay, Ontario, Canada	7
32	David Anton	Mount Laurel, New Jersey	7
32	Timothy Stevens	Wells, Maine	7
35	Timothy Penasack	Nashua, New Hampshire	6
35	Tom Ottey	Columbus, Ohio	6
37	Chris Whiteman	Clinton Twp., Michigan	4
37	Eric Burmeister	Dearborn Hts., Michigan	4
39	Mark Tabor	West Linn, Oregon	3
39	Don Jankowski	Lake Orion, Michigan	3
39	Amy BeberVanzo	Petaluma, California	3
39	Brooks Freehill	Boulder, Colorado	3
43	Dave Hintz	Enumclaw, Washington	2
44	Seamus Burke	Powder Springs, Georgia	1
44	J. B. Niday	Richfield, Minnesota	1
44	Fintan Seeley	Park Ridge, New Jersey	1
44	Jimmy Keeney	Colorado Springs, Colorado	1
44	Patrick Moro	Dublin, Ohio	1
44	Derek Bottles	Seattle, Washington	1
44	Marek Podoluch	Romeoville, Illinois	1

Co-Driver

#	Name	Home Base	Points
28	Jeff Secor	Hudsonville, Michigan	6
28	Marc Goldfarb	Atkinson, New Hampshire	6
28	Mike Rossey	Rochester, Minnesota	6
31	Conrad Ketelsen	Shakopee, Minnesota	5
31	Stephan Duffy	Yonkers, New York	5
33	Dave Shindle	Falls Church, Virginia	4
33	Marc McAllister	Woodside, New York	4
35	Mark Larson	Blaine, Minnesota	3
35	Charles Bradley	Kennesaw, Georgia	3
35	Claire Chizma	Seattle, Washington	3
35	Tim Sardelich	Orangevale, California	3
35	Kevin Poirier	Rainier, Oregon	3
40	Rick Hintz	El Cajon, California	2
41	Jason Grahn	Federal Way, Washington	1
41	Paddy McCague	Bronx, New York	1
41	David Kean	Everett, Washington	1
41	Matthew Collins	Chicago, Illinois	1
41	Adam Pelc	Middle Village, New York	1
41	Kazimierz Pudelek	Chicago, Illinois	1

Rally America Championship

Class Positions

Driver			
Open			
#	Name	Home Base	Points
1	Matthew Iorio	Millis, Massachusetts	124
2	James Cox	Hamel, Minnesota	64
3	Chris Gilligan	Cornelius, North Carolina	52
4	George Plsek Jr.	Del Mar, California	37
5	Martin Donnelly	Pearl River, New York	29
6	Robert Olson	Eden Prairie, Minnesota	27
7	Tom Ottey	Columbus, Ohio	26
8	Ramana Lagemann	Somerville, Massachusetts	23
9	Stephan Verdier	Huntington Beach, California	22
10	Tim Paterson	Redmond, Washington	19
10	Douglas Havir	Golden Valley, Minnesota	19
12	Doug Shepherd	Plymouth, Michigan	14
12	Amy BeberVanzo	Petaluma, California	14
12	Henry Krolikowski	Wyandotte, Michigan	14
15	Dave Hintz	Enumclaw, Washington	2
16	Fintan Seeley	Park Ridge, New Jersey	1
16	Marek Podoluch	Romeoville, Illinois	1
16	Seamus Burke	Powder Springs, Georgia	1
16	J. B. Niday	Richfield, Minnesota	1

Co-Driver			
Open			
#	Name	Home Base	Points
1	Ole Holter	Long Beach, California	119
2	Joe Petersen	Rubicon, Wisconsin	52
3	Jeffrey Burmeister	St. Louis Park, Minnesota	45
4	John Allen	Bainbridge Island, Washington	37
5	Jeffrey Becker	New York, New York	23
6	Pamela McGarvey	Columbus, Ohio	20
7	Jason Gillespie	Maspeth, New York	18
8	John Dillon	Thousand Oaks, California	17
9	Cynthia Krolikowski	Wyandotte, Michigan	14
9	Pete Gladysz	Troy, Michigan	14
11	Stephan Duffy	Yonkers, New York	12
11	Mark Larson	Blaine, Minnesota	12
11	Conrad Ketelsen	Shakopee, Minnesota	12
11	Tim Sardelich	Orangevale, California	12
15	Marc McAllister	Woodside, New York	10
15	Claire Chizma	Seattle, Washington	10
17	Charles Bradley	Kennesaw, Georgia	8
18	Rick Hintz	El Cajon, California	2
19	David Kean	Everett, Washington	1
19	Paddy McCague	Bronx, New York	1
19	Kazimierz Pudelek	Chicago, Illinois	1
19	Marc Goldfarb	Atkinson, New Hampshire	1
19	Noel Gallagher	Yonkers, New York	1

Rally America Championship
Class Positions

Driver

Group N

#	Name	Home Base	Points
1	Patrick Richard	Garibaldi Highlands, B.C., Can.	124
2	Stig Blomqvist	Northants, United Kingdom	122
3	Ken Block	Encinitas, California	79
4	Travis Pastrana	Annapolis, Maryland	73
5	Mark Utecht	Stacy, Minnesota	36
6	Mark McElduff	Chicago, Illinois	34
7	Otis Dimiters	Great Neck, New York	31
8	Jonathan Bottoms	Buffalo, New York	28
9	Wyeth Gubelmann	Placerville, Colorado	25
10	David Anton	Mount Laurel, New Jersey	23
11	Henry Krolikowski	Wyandotte, Michigan	22
11	Fintan McCarthy	Chicago, Illinois	22
13	William Bacon	Chelmsford, Massachusetts	20
14	Lauchlin O'Sullivan	San Francisco, California	14

Production GT

#	Name	Home Base	Points
1	Tanner Foust	Steamboat Springs, Colorado	124
2	Matthew Johnson	Apex, North Carolina	112
3	Eric Langbein	Potomac, Maryland	100
4	Timothy Stevens	Wells, Maine	30
5	Joan Hoskinson	Thunder Bay, Ontario, Canada	29
6	Timothy Penasack	Nashua, New Hampshire	20
7	Robert Olson	Eden Prairie, Minnesota	1
7	Patrick Moro	Dublin, Ohio	1
7	Stephan Verdier	Huntington Beach, California	1

Co-Driver

Group N

#	Name	Home Base	Points
1	Nathalie Richard	St-Jean-sur-Richelieu, Q.C. Canada	129
2	Ana Goni	Northants, United Kingdom	100
3	Christian Edstrom	New York, New York	85
4	Alessandro Gelsomino	Santa Clarita, California	78
5	Cynthia Krolikowski	Wyandotte, Michigan	49
6	Rob Bohn	Noblesville, Indiana	36
7	Peter Monin	Norwalk, Connecticut	31
8	Carolyn Bosley	Hinesburg, Vermont	30
9	Noel Gallagher	Yonkers, New York	25
10	Peter Watt	Peterborough, Ontario, Canada	20
11	John Dillon	Thousand Oaks, California	14
12	Andrew Coombs	Mercerville, New Jersey	13
13	Mike Rossey	Rochester, Michigan	10
14	Matthew Collins	Chicago, Illinois	1

Production GT

#	Name	Home base	Points
1	Scott Crouch	Boulder, Colorado	124
2	Wendy Nakamoto	Sacramento, California	112
3	Jeremy Wimpey	Herndon, Virginia	100
4	Jeff Secor	Hudsonville, Michigan	31
5	Marc Goldfarb	Atkinson, New Hampshire	19
6	Conrad Ketelsen	Shakopee, Minnesota	1
6	Jimmy Brandt	Lake Odessa, Michigan	1

Rally America Championship
Class Positions

Driver

Group 5

#	Name	Home Base	Points
1	Doug Shepherd	Plymouth, Michigan	66
2	Bruce Davis	Granite Bay, California	36
3	Brooks Freehill	Boulder, Colorado	22
4	Chris Whiteman	Clinton Twp, Michigan	18
5	Eric Burmeister	Dearborn Hts, Michigan	15
6	Mark Utecht	Stacy, Minnesota	1

Group 2

#	Name	Home Base	Points
1	Matt Johnston	Rockford, Michigan	88
2	Derek Bottles	Seattle, Washington	1
2	Jimmy Keeney	Colorado Springs, Colorado	1

Production

#	Name	Home Base	Points
1	Sans Thompson	Grass Valley, California	84
2	Michael Merbach	Appleton, Wisconsin	56
3	Mark Tabor	West Linn, Oregon	22
3	Don Jankowski	Lake Orion, Michigan	22

Co-Driver

Group 5

#	Name	Home Base	Points
1	Jimmy Brandt	Lake Odessa, Michigan	38
2	Pete Gladysz	Troy, Michigan	22
2	Mike Rossey	Rochester, Michigan	22
4	Dave Shindle	Falls Church, Virginia	18
5	John Dillon	Thousand Oaks, California	1
5	Rob Bohn	Noblesville, Indiana	1

Group 2

#	Name	Home Base	Points
1	Alexander Kihurani	Mohnton, Pennsylvania	88
2	Jason Grahn	Federal Way, Washington	1
2	Adam Pelc	Middle Village, New York	1

Production

#	Name	Home Base	Points
1	Craig Marr	Chico, California	84
2	Jeff Feldt	Kaukauna, Wisconsin	61
3	Kevin Poirier	Rainier, Oregon	22

United States Rally Championship
Overall Positions

#	Driver Name	Points		#	Co-Driver Name	Points
1	Tom Lawless	108		1	Jason Gillespie	108
2	Matthew Iorio	86		2	Ole Holter	86
3	Peter Workum	79		3	Christine Beavis	79
4	Seamus Burke	62		4	Jason Grahn	53
5	Craig Hollingsworth	53		5	Stephen Duffy	46
6	Danny O'Brien	46		6	Jimmy Brandt	39
7	Pat Richard	36		7	Nathalie Richard	36
8	Ken Block	35		8	Eddie Fries	35
9	Sam Murray	31		9	Brian Sharky	31
10	Bruce Davis	31		9	Anton Cheetham	31
11	Jimmy Keeney	30		11	Alex Gelsomino	31
12	Patrick Lilly	28		12	Brian Moody	30
12	Stephan Verdier	28		13	Bernard Farrell	28
14	Emilio Arce	26		14	Allan Walker	24
15	Matthew Johnson	22		15	Craig Thrall	22
15	Mike Whitman	22		15	Wendy Nakamoto	22
17	Blake Yoon	22		15	Bill Westrick	22
17	Lisa Klassen	22		18	Jay Socha	22
17	Erik Lyden	22		18	John Dillon	22
20	Darrell Pugh	20		20	Dominik Jozwiak	20
20	Maciej Przybysz	20		20	Jonathan Barnes	20
20	Ralph Kosmides	20		20	Andrew Cushman	20
20	Dennis Chizma	20		23	Russell Strate	18
24	Randy Zimmer	18		24	Amity Trowbridge	17
25	Donald Kennedy	17		24	Keith Kennedy	17
25	Bill Malik	17		26	Kim DeMotte	17
27	Jeff Rados	15		27	Lee Sorenson	16

United States Rally Championship

Overall Positions

Driver			Co-Driver		
#	Name	Points	#	Name	Points
29	Josh Chang	14	28	Noel Gallagher	16
29	Doug Robinson	14	29	Guido Hamacher	15
31	Justin Pritchard	13	29	Casey Blust	15
31	Marvin Ronquillo	13	31	Alex Kihurani	14
31	Mike Masano	13	31	Sue Robinson	14
34	Cyril Kearney	12	33	John Burke	13
34	Brad Morris	12	33	Linda Masano	13
36	Larry Gross	11	35	Ryan Gutile	12
37	Doug Chernis	10	36	Doug Young	11
38	Flip Van Zutphen	9	37	Alan Perry	10
39	Nick Hudson	8	38	Theo Badenberg	9
40	Patrick Farrell	8	39	Brian Hudson	8
40	Leon Styles	8	40	Kieran McElhinney	8
40	Brian Yee	4	40	Mark McAllister	8
40	Eric Heitkamp	4	42	Kala Rounds	7
40	Greg Gilfeather	4	43	Brian Ockwell	4
40	Hampton Bridwell	4	43	Robbie Durant	4
40	John Buffum	4	43	Robert Amato	4
40	Joshua Wimpey	4	43	Samantha Smyth	4
40	Liam Egan	4	43	William Sekella	4
40	Mark Bowers	4	43	Jim Brandt	4
40	Mark Spence	4	43	Alex Gelsomino	4
40	Martin Donnelly	4	43	Abel Villesca	4
40	Scott Gardner	4	43	Amar Sehmi	4
40	Sean Coffey	4	43	Brian Coats	4
40	Noel Nash	4	43	Brian McGuire	4

United States Rally Championship

Overall Positions

Driver				Co-Driver		
#	Name	Points		#	Name	Points
40	Otis Dimitiers	4		43	Cindy Krolikowski	4
40	Brian Scott	4		43	David Hackett	4
40	Brooks Freehill	4		43	Jeff Burmeister	4
40	Chad Dykes	4		43	Andrew Jessup	4
40	Dennis Martin	4		43	Andrew Troyell	4
40	George Plsek	4		43	Charlie Bradley	4
40	Jim Pierce	4		43	Chris Wallpe	4
40	Victor Kuhns	4		43	Constantine Montopolus	4
40	Wolfgang Hoeck	4		43	Declan Brady	4
40	Wyeth Gubelmann	4		43	Duffy Bowers	4
40	Bruce Davis	4		43	Jeremy Wimpey	4
40	Cyril Kearney	4		43	Josh Katinger	4
40	David Anton	4		43	Mark Williams	4
40	Donal McGivney	4		43	Rick Davis	4
40	Robin Jones	4		43	Sarah Gardescu	4
40	Cem Akdeniz	4		43	Sean Moriarty	4
40	Marco Pasten	4		43	Mustafa Samli	4
40	Tony Chavez	4		43	Jennifer Imai	4
40	Scott Clark	4		43	Bret Robinson	4
40	Christopher Hill	4		43	Alan Ockwell	4
				43	Marie Boyd	4
				43	Clover Sonnentag	4

United States Rally Championship
Class Positions

Driver		
Open 4-Wheel Drive		

#	Name	Points
1	Thomas Lawless	108
2	Peter Workum	84
3	Seamus Burke	66
4	Matthew Iorio	62
5	Pat Richard	36
6	Eric Lyden	31
7	Patrick Lilly	28
8	Mike Whitman	27
9	Danny O'Brien	24
10	Blake Yoon	24
11	Darrell Pugh	22
12	Maciej Przybysz	22
13	Randy Zimmer	20
14	Flip Van Zutphen	20
15	Donald Kennedy	18
15	Martin Donnelly	4
15	Leon Styles	8
16	Liam Egan	4
16	Scott Gardner	4
16	Mark Bowers	4
16	John Buffum	4
16	Geroge Plsek	4
16	Jim Pierce	4
16	Chad Dykes	4
16	Noel Nash	4
16	Patrick Farrell	4

Co-Driver		
Open 4-Wheel Drive		

#	Name	Points
1	Jason Gillespie	108
2	Christine Beavis	84
3	Ole Holter	62
4	Eddie Fries	39
5	Nathalie Richard	36
6	Brian Sharkey	31
7	Jay Socha	31
8	Bernard Farrell	28
9	Bill Westrick	27
10	Stephan Duffy	24
11	John Dillon	24
12	Jonathan Barnes	22
13	Dominik Jozwiak	22
14	Russell Strate	20
15	Theo Bradenberg	20
16	Keith Kennedy	18
17	Mark McAllister	8
18	Charles Bradley	4
18	Sean Moriarty	4
18	Constantine Mantopolas	4
18	Duffy Bowers	4
18	Mark Williams	4
18	Jeff Burmiester	4
18	Amar Sehmi	4
18	Brian Coats	4
18	Kierian McElhinney	4

United States Rally Championship
Class Positions

Driver				Co-Driver		

Driver

Open 4-Wheel Drive

#	Name	Points
16	Blake Yoon	4
16	Cyril Kearney	4
16	Stephan Verdier	4
16	Scott Clark	4

Group N

1	Ken Block	44
2	Sam Murray	36
3	Mathew Iorio	31
4	Ralph Kosmides	31
5	Doug Chernis	27
6	Wyeth Gubelman	4
6	Wolfgang Heck	4
6	Victor Kuhns	4
6	Otis Demiters	4
6	David Anton	4
6	Clem Akdeniz	4
6	Mustafa Samli	4

Open 2-Wheel Drive

1	Craig Hollingsworth	103
2	Bruce Davis	62
3	Jimmy Keeney	60
4	Lisa Klassen	50
5	Bill Malik	36
6	Jeff Rados	31

Co-Driver

Open 4-Wheel Drive

#	Name	Points
18	Robert Amato	4
18	Samantha Smyth	4
18	Alan Oakwell	4
18	Marie Boyd	4

Group N

1	Alex Gelsomino	44
2	Anton Cheetham	36
3	Ole Holter	31
4	Jimmy Brandt	31
5	Alan Perry	27
6	Cindy Krolikowski	4
6	John Dillon	4
6	Abel Villesca	4
6	Alan Ockwell	4
6	Robbie Durant	4
6	Mustafa Samli	4

Open 2-Wheel Drive

1	Jason Grahn	99
2	Amity Trowbridge	36
3	Brian Moody	36
4	Jimmy Brandt	35
5	Lee Sorenson	31
6	Guido Hamacher	31

United States Rally Championship

Class Positions

Driver				Co-Driver		

Open 2-Wheel Drive

#	Name	Points
7	Justin Pritchard	27
7	Brad Morris	27
9	Larry Gross	24
10	Dennis Martin	4
10	Brian Scott	4
10	Books Freehill	4
10	Sean Coffey	4
10	Robin Jones	4
10	Bruce Davis	4
10	Marco Pasten	4

Open 2-Wheel Drive

#	Name	Points
7	Kim DeMotte	31
8	Casey Blust	28
9	Ryan Gutile	27
10	Brian Moody	24
11	Doug Youg	24
12	Kala Rounds	22
13	Declan Brady	4
13	David Hackett	4
13	Brian McGurie	4
13	William Sekella	4
13	Jennifer Imai	4
13	Jason Grahn	4

Grand Touring

#	Name	Points
1	Danny O'Brien	36
2	Cyril Kearney	31
3	Patrick Farrell	4

Grand Touring

#	Name	Points
1	Stephen Duffy	36
2	Noel Gallagher	31
3	Kieran McElhinney	4

United States Rally Championship
Class Positions

	Driver				Co-Driver	

Driver — **Super Stock**

#	Name	Points
1	Emilo Arce	40
2	Stephan Verdie	36
3	Dennis Chizma	36
4	Josh Chang	36
5	Matthew Johnson	31
6	Nick Hudson	31
7	Marvin Ronquillo	27
8	Hampton Bridwell	4
8	Greg Gilfeather	4
8	Donal McGivney	4
8	Christopher Hill	4

Driver — **Stock**

#	Name	Points
1	Doug Robinson	36
2	Mike Masano	31
3	Eric Heitkamp	4
3	Tony Chavez	4

Co-Driver — **Super Stock**

#	Name	Points
1	Allan Walker	36
2	Craig Thrall	36
3	Andrew Cushman	36
4	Alex Kihurani	36
5	Wendy Nakamoto	31
6	Brian Hudson	31
7	John Burke	27
8	Sarah Gardescu	4
8	Josh Katinger	4
8	Rick Davis	4
8	Noel Gallagher	4
8	Colver Sonnentag	4

Co-Driver — **Stock**

#	Name	Points
1	Sue Robinson	36
2	Linda Masano	31
3	Andrew Jessup	4
3	Bret Robinson	4

Organizational Contacts

	Location	Web Address
<u>Rally America Championship</u>		www.rally-america.com
Sno*Drift Rally	Atlanta, Michigan	www.sno-drift.org
Ojibwe Forests Rally	Bemidji, Minnesota	www.ojibweforestrally.com
Falken Tire Pikes Peak International Hill Climb	Colorado Springs, Colorado	www.ppihc.com
Oregon Trail Rally	Hillsboro, Oregon	www.oregontrailrally.com
Lake Superior Pro Rally (LSPR)	Houghton, Michigan	www.lsprorally.com
Maine Forest Rally	Bethel, Maine	www.maineforestrally.com
Colorado Cog Rally	Steamboat Springs, Colorado	www.coloradocogrally.com
Susquehannock Trail Pro Rally (STPR)	Wellsboro, Pennsylvania	www.stpr.org
<u>United States Rally Championship</u>		www.unitedstatesrallychampionship.com
Cherokee Trails International Rally	Chattanooga, Tenessee	www.cherokeetrailsrally.com
Subaru Rim of the World Rally	Lancaster, California	www.rimoftheworldrally.com
Ramada Express International Rally	Laughlin, Nevada	www.rallyusa.com
International Rally New York	Monticello, New York	www.rallynewyork.com
<u>World Rally Championship</u>		www.wrc.com
Corona Rally México	León, México	www.rallymexico.com

<u>SPEED-PICS</u>

To purchase additional copies of this book, please contact your original supplier or write to:

SPEED-PICS Publishing   www.speed-pics.com
6101 Long Prairie Road, #744-110
Flower Mound, TX 75028

About the Author

After gaining a degree from Queen's University, Belfast (United Kingdom), Ronnie Arnold spent over twenty-five years in the technology industry. His experience ranges from ten years as a consultant based in Belfast and London to being chief technology officer for a startup in Silicon Valley, California.

Recently he changed career to focus on his long-term passion of photography, specializing in motor sport—rallies and road races.

His interest in motor sport started in Northern Ireland where he competed as a driver and co-driver in regional rally and sprint events—gaining his International Rally Driver's License in the early 1970s.

He was a member of council and press officer for the Ulster Automobile Club (best known for the Circuit of Ireland International Rally). He edited the club's *Wheelspin* magazine, was a member of the competitions committee and was heavily involved in the organization of the circuit.

His images have been published in magazines, newspapers and on Web sites.

Arnold lives in Highland Village, Texas. He is a member of the Professional Photographers of America.